PAKISTAN

To:
Dear Tabeen & Iqbal Ali.
With compliments.
from
K. Tausif Kamal;
McKinney, Texas 5/24/2021

PAKISTAN

A Possible Future

K. TAUSIF KAMAL

ARCHWAY PUBLISHING

Archway Publishing books may be ordered through booksellers or by contacting:

Archway Publishing
1663 Liberty Drive
Bloomington, IN 47403
www.archwaypublishing.com
1 (888) 242-5904

ISBN: 978-1-4808-8409-0 (sc)
ISBN: 978-1-4808-8408-3 (hc)
ISBN: 978-1-4808-8410-6 (e)

Library of Congress Control Number: 2019917835

Print information available on the last page.

Archway Publishing rev. date: 01/02/2020

Other Works by the Author

K. Tausif Kamal, *U.S. Immigration Laws: How to Apply*
(Chapel Hill, NC: Professional Press, 1994),
US Library of Congress: ISBN-13-978-1880365885.

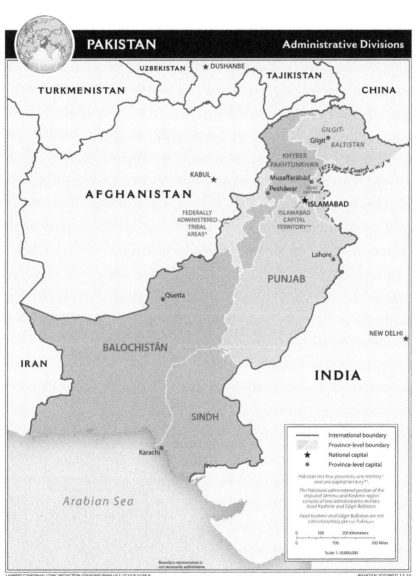

PAKISTAN   Administrative Divisions

UZBEKISTAN   ★ DUSHANBE
TAJIKISTAN
TURKMENISTAN   CHINA

                                              GILGIT-
                                        Gilgit ⊛ BALTISTAN
                                    KHYBER
                                    PAKHTUNKHWA
                                              1972 Line of Control
                        KABUL   Muzaffarābād ⊛
                          ★   Peshāwar ⊛   AZAD
AFGHANISTAN   KASHMIR
                                                ★ISLAMABAD
                        FEDERALLY   ISLAMABAD
                        ADMINISTERED   CAPITAL
                        TRIBAL   TERRITORY**
                        AREAS*
                                            Lahore ⊛

                                        PUNJAB
               Quetta ⊛
                                                            NEW DELHI
                                                                ★
        BALOCHISTĀN
IRAN
                                                        INDIA

                        SINDH

            Karachi ⊛

    Arabian Sea

                                        ┌─────────────────────────────────┐
                                        │ ───── International boundary   │
                                        │   Province-level boundary   │
                                        │ ★   National capital   │
                                        │ ⊛   Province-level capital   │
                                        │ Pakistan has four provinces, one territory*, │
                                        │ and one capital territory**.   │
                                        │ The Pakistani-administered portion of the │
                                        │ disputed Jammu and Kashmir region   │
                                        │ consists of two administrative entities: │
                                        │ Azad Kashmir and Gilgit-Baltistan. │
                                        │ Azad Kashmir and Gilgit-Baltistan are not │
                                        │ constitutionally part of Pakistan. │
                                        │ 0   100   200 Kilometers   │
                                        │ 0   100   200 Miles   │
                                        │   Scale 1:10,000,000   │
                                        └─────────────────────────────────┘
            Boundary representation is
            not necessarily authoritative.

LAMBERT CONFORMAL CONIC PROJECTION; STANDARD PARALLELS 23°33' N 35°44' N   803473AI (G02807) 12-10

Dedication

For the agonized people of Pakistan.

And for my late mother, Bilquis Jehan Begum, the most amazing, loving woman in my life.

Contents

Foreword

Pakistan is world's sixth largest country with a population of 212 million people and a land mass of 881,913 square kilometers, including a coastline of about a thousand kilometers on the Arabian Sea and Gulf of Oman. It's also the world's second largest state in terms of population- after Indonesia. Its landscape is as diverse as its ethnic people, areas ranging from the stunning mountainous beauty of the northwest province of Khyber Pashtun Khwa province (KPK) and the Gilgit-Hunza (GB) regions in the northeast to the fertile plains of Panjab province and rugged hills of Balochistan province to the deserts of Sindh province. Islamabad is the capital city, but Karachi is its biggest city. It's a nuclear-powered country with the world's sixth largest army and a per capita income of about $1,500 per year.

Rich in history and tradition, Pakistan is home of one of world's oldest civilization, the 1,700 BC Mohenjadaro (a UNESCO's World Heritage site) and Harrapa civilization in Sindh and Panjab provinces that are part of the overarching Indus Valley civilization of the country. Majestic River Indus is the country's artery. Originating in the northern mountain ranges it, along with its five tributaries, flows through the plains of Panjab and Sindh into the Arabian Sea, providing a lifeline of water for fertile agriculture. Karakoram mountain rage in the north has some of world's highest peaks including the second highest K-2 peak (28,000 feet) and scenic beauty in Swat, Hunza, Gilgit and Baltistan region.

Pakistan was established on August 14, 1947, after the bloody partition of India by Britain as a result of demand for a separate and independent homeland for the Muslims of India by the Muslim League Party, which was spearheaded by Mohammad Ali Jinnah, its founding father. [1] It has had an eventful, unstable political history because of wars with India, military coups, and experiments in democracy. [2] In the 1971 war with India, its eastern wing separated from the country and created an independent and sovereign country, Bangladesh. [3,4,5]

In 1958, its first military coup was executed by General Ayub Khan, who then ruled as president. Subsequently in 1977, the popularly elected Prime Minster Z. A. Bhutto was deposed and hanged by General Zia ul Haq who brought a rigid Islamist rule. In 1988, Benazir Bhutto became its prime minister, the first Muslim woman in the Islamic world to achieve this status, but tragically, she was assassinated in a terrorist bombing in 2007. General Parvez Musharraf seized power in 2001 through a coup overthrowing the democratic government of Prime Minister Nawaz Sharif. After a series of judiciary's improper removals and disqualifications of elected prime ministers, Nawaz Sharif and Yusuf Gilani, general elections were held in 2018, and they installed chief of PTI party, Imran Khan, as the current prime minister.

Pakistan is basically an agricultural country producing and exporting cotton, wheat rice, sugarcane, and other crops. However, it's gradually transforming itself into a partially industrialized nation. Its national language is Urdu, though it has four regional languages— Panjabi, Sindhi, Balochi, and Pushto.

CHAPTER 1

Crisis Galore

This book is not about Pakistan's past but rather about its future—a possible future, not a guaranteed future. As such, it's not intended for just the cognoscenti but for the people at large.

Viable or Not

"Pakistan is a country full of riddles," says noted historian of Pakistan Ayesha Jalal in her book *The Struggle for Pakistan*. As she puts it, "It is a state which was created out of confusion and contradictions, and a state yet to build up a nation within." [1] Yes, the enigma of Pakistan endures and continues, though a bit falteringly.

Even after a span of seventy years of Pakistan's existence as a nation-state, the fact that questions of its continued viability are still being raised is an indication of the politically shaky grounds the country stands on. In the scholarly words of Jalal, "The logic of its creation and the causes of its survival are two questions that need to be answered by scholars of generations." True that the logic of its creation is yet to be conclusively established: it's still being debated. But the second query about the causes of country's survival is akin to begging the question. After all, the country has survived through wars, natural disasters such as earthquakes and floods, famines, wars, the separation of half of its region, near bankruptcy, destructive religious fanaticism, bloodthirsty terrorism, military coups, Indo-Pak wars, and political dysfunction.

The country's constitution is under siege, a far cry from being a unifying and inspiring lodestar for its besieged citizens. However, the lugubrious landscape of the nation does not necessarily spell its doom. Its continuity against unfavorable odds demonstrates its resiliency and survival skills. Having reached another inflection point in its national journey, we must ask if the country will be able to successfully navigate the machinations of its rulers ensorcelled by power and pelf?

Through a certain kind of resiliency and remnant nationalism, Pakistan has continued on its dogged and, as some would say, foolhardy existence as a nation-state, even though beset by formidable challenges that are topped by some burgeoning existential threats highlighted below;

Five Existential Threats

1. Terrorism: Both the domestic and cross-border variety of terrorism is a huge threat for the country's political sovereignty, and this existential threat that is not going away. The former has caused thousands of deaths and destruction and destabilized the country while the latter has triggered hostilities with Pakistan's neighboring nations. It has ignited border hostilities with Afghanistan and Iran and wars with India.

2. Ethnic uprisings: Broadly speaking, there are four ethnic uprisings in various stages. The Baloch uprising is the hottest one with its BLA (Balochistan Liberation Army) and other wings. The nonviolent Pashtun resentment in FATA and KPK is captured by the growing PTM (Pashtun Tahafuz Movement). Ethnic discontent in Sindh is simmering in its urban areas by the MQM Party (Muttahida Qaumi Movement) and the Sindh nationalist groups in rural Sindh.

3. Population growth rate: Pakistan's 2% growth rate of its population is among the highest in the world. even twice that of its teeming neighbors, India and Bangladesh. Its estimated

that its population will double by 2050, a recipe for existential disaster given its limited resources. [2]

4. Water scarcity: So severe is the country's water problem that currently its listed as being in a water crisis. Available water per capita on an annual basis has been reduced from 1,500 cubic feet in 2009 to 1,000 cubic feet in 2018. Its predicted that Pakistan would face a drought level water crisis by the year 2025 if drastic steps are not taken to resolve it. [3]

5. Debt and poverty: Pakistan is drowning in debts and liabilities. Its total public debt, which includes external debt of about $100 billion, is about 70 percent of its annual GDP. About forty-five million of its people are barely living below the poverty line and earning less than two dollars per day. Its economic indicators are reaching a tipping point when one looks at the continued viability of the state. [4,5]

CHAPTER 2

Moving Forward

If you're going through hell, keep going.
—Winston Churchill

Though Pakistan is not exactly going through hell, there is no doubt that its going through a very tough time, and as stated, its only path is forward. Standing still, stuck in the wet concrete of the past, and conducting business as usual is not an option. For future survival Pakistan must strive forward and change along the direction of a non-revisionist, nonviolent, peaceful, tolerant, moderate, market-oriented, modern nation-state. Innovation, reformation, [1] new ideas, and new ways of looking at things along with incremental and pragmatic approaches are all needed, and this book outlines such an attempt. [2]

Blueprint for Possible Success

Chapter 1 (Crisis Galore) highlights the core problems facing the country, while chapter 2 (Moving Forward), chapter 3 (Introspection: Assault on the Constitution), chapter 4 (Correcting the Constitution), chapter 5 (Pakistani Welfare Nationalism), chapter 6 (Reforming the Institutions), chapter 7 (Fighting Terrorism and Extremism), chapter 8 (Strategizing the Economy), chapter 9 (Modernizing the Environment), chapter 10 (Changing State Policy), chapter 11 (Food for Thought), chapter 12 (Conclusion), and the Epilogue point to a balanced, pragmatic, and possible way to achieve the objectives of growth, prosperity, and viability of a transformed modern Pakistan state.

No Revolution

Some say that the decay in the country and its institutions is total, and since the cancer has engulfed the entire system, a complete transplantation of a successful model from a foreign nation is needed. But the country might not be able to survive this radical surgery given the precarious condition of the patient. A better analogy is to repair the decadent national denture one tooth at a time so that the country can begin to bite again. Some institutional teeth may just need cleansing. Others may need filings in the cavities, and other seriously rotten institutions may require root canals. Still, those beyond repair would have to be extracted, and new institutional models may need to be implanted in their places.

In the same vein that the country's institutions are beyond repair, its socioeconomic system and political order are beyond redemption, some call for a full-fledged revolution in the country, a complete rejection of the constitution, and an overthrow of all social and economic institutions resulting in a massive, fundamental transformation of society. Some blame the half-hearted, haphazard application of the so-called Pakistan ideology (read Islamic) for the ills of the country. However, the era of revolutions and ideologies seems to be on the wane. The last full-scale revolution was Iran's Islamic Revolution in 1970s, and look what it has done to the lives of people there. Furthermore, this era of ideologies seems to be over as witnessed by the failure of socialism in Russia and elsewhere.

Effective Democracy

Pakistan is in the process of discovering that holding periodic elections do not constitute democracy. Elections are no doubt its important facet, but they are the means, not an end. A restrained but effective democracy is the call of the hour for Pakistan.[6] The goal of a democracy, restrained or not, is to have a representative government that is responsive to the needs of the people, that delivers the public good, that provides progress and prosperity, and that serves the interests of the citizens and the state. How the country can move forward and possibly meet this overriding challenge is recommended in the following chapters. These measures include streamlining Pakistan's various institutions and governance in a phased approach; adopting a dynamic, motivational, and aspiring nationalism (Pakistan welfare nationalism); implementing new constructive and rewarding foreign and security policy; modernizing the social environment; executing a market-oriented economic strategy; and eviscerating the scourge of terrorism and extremism.

Pakistani democracy is a very fragile plant that needs constant vigilance and nurturing. Steven Levitsky and Daniel Zibleth (*How Democracies Die*) contend, "Democracies die not only though military coercion but also at the hands of its elected rulers."[7] This maxim has been so true in the case of Pakistan. Saplings of democracy along with people's hopes and aspirations for its growth have not only been quashed by military coups and generals' greed but have also been subverted by elected rulers. It's a lesson that must be learned by the civilian rulers as well.

For a democratic order to sustain itself and flourish, constitutional rule and strong institutions, though essential requirements, are not enough without the prevalence of the values, practices, and norms of democracy.[5] As the democratic norms in a society, including free debates, discussion of issues in the marketplace of ideas, tolerance of dissenting views, and a respect for law and the rights of others, wither away, so does democracy. Pakistan's greatest challenge would be to build a tolerant, progressive, multiethnic order based on political and social equality of all citizens, guided and spearheaded by visionary and sincere political leaders. As the renowned intellectual and commentator Charles Krauthammer cautioned, "Politics is the moat, the walls beyond which lie the barbarians. Failure to keep them at bay, everything burns."[11] Identity politics, whether that is s based on ethnicity of Panjab, Sindh, KPK Balochistan or Mohajirs, or based on religious sects, Sunni, Shia,

Deobandi, Barelvi, etc. must be shunned or discussed in matters of national interest, as it gives rise to partisan polarization in the country. An overarching national identity of being a Pakistani first must be adhered to.

Strategy is defined as "maintaining a balance ... between the means and methods available for meeting (identified) objectives" (Lawrence Freedman) [3] This book is such an attempt to maintain this balance while decisively transforming Pakistan from a security state into a modern, peaceful, tolerant, progressive, market-oriented, welfare state.

Free Speech and Media

Without freedom of speech and press, an effective democracy cannot take root. When the print and electronic media of Pakistan is made to function as a tool to propagate a specific narrative of an unrepresentative institution, the country's faltering march toward a democratic order would further suffer. Media reports of *election engineering* and meddling in politics were no secret. The attacks on the free media have been execrable and unjustifiable and Kafkaesque in nature at times. The very purpose of a free media, namely to foster free debate and frank discussion of national issues, challenge any ideology, and find solutions, would be defeated if the country's military establishment persists in its endeavor to manipulate and control media and public opinions directly through force, brutality, coercion, arrests, disappearance, and assassinations or indirectly via self-censorship, the stoppage of advertisements, the disruption of newspaper distributions, the severing of TV cable connections, and other methods. Furthermore, recourse to such coercive actions to silence dissent and free expression would inevitably result in the military losing peoples' trust and squandering whatever goodwill it has generated throughout the years.

Learning from the Past

In order to move forward, a nation must learn from its past history. The lessons it attempts to learn and adopt for future dispensation must be learned with an open mind that's not enslaved by preconceived ideas, beliefs, and traditions. Otherwise, the whole process will defeat the very purpose of such an exercise. Doctors first study the medical history of a patient before prescribing a course for future treatment. The history of military warfare and battles fought in the past are taught to military officers and strategists in military academies around the world so that in the event of a conflict, they can avoid military mistakes that previous generals made. Pakistan must first identify and acknowledge the blunders its leaders and society have committed in the past seventy years, draw lessons from their mistakes, and then move forward by filtering and applying lessons gleaned from its history.

The nation can begin the redeeming process by asking itself some vital questions. Have the endless hostilities with its big and booming neighbor, India, helped or hindered Pakistan in achieving national security and economic progress? Has the strategy to use proxy militant groups served the country's national interest, security, and international image or reputation? If so, how? Has its policy of sole reliance on external aid and sources for achieving economic prosperity without a dedicated national endeavor for development achieved its objectives? Has its tackling of ethnic uprisings in Balochistan, KPK, and Sindh regions resulted in the permanent settlement of these crises and promotion of national cohesion and unity? If so, how? Have civil society and the authorities sinking deeper and deeper into fundamentalism and supremacism achieved social and economic well-being of the people and created a peaceful, tolerant, dynamic country? Were any of the three- or five-year national economic and developments plans adopted and successfully implemented to completion?

The answer to these fundamental questions is a resounding no, which is a sobering thought for those passionate citizens who want to see a prosperous Pakistan. The negative responses indicate that it's time to jettison these failed policies, approaches, and beliefs. It's not rocket science. It's simply time to move on from these policies.

Nation Rebuilding

The exercise of reforming or rebuilding a nation is easier said than done. It's no easy and simple task. It involves building up infrastructure along with political and social engineering on a massive scale with all the attendant complexities, sacrifices, and challenges. In the case of Pakistan, being a partially developed country, it's not devoid of any physical infrastructure. As such, rebuilding or reforming the nation rather than a ground-level building is needed. But whatever any improvement or streamlining efforts are termed as, they will be hampered without question by the debilitating expenditure on defense, especially given the billions of dollars that are spent on purchasing the latest arms and weapons, which comprises a big chunk of country's external debt of $105 billion. What makes this problem more acute is the fact that Pakistan has a dwarf economy (barely $300 billion total GDP) with a very low growth rate. The burgeoning defense expenditures syphon away a large part of capital that could have been employed for infrastructure projects.

Besides the economic and physical aspects of nation building in Pakistan, two other ingredients are essential to inculcate—hard work and modernization. The nation's prevailing ubiquitous culture of prayers to high heaven and wishful thinking must be replaced by imbibing high ethical values of hard work and true dedication. Moreover, the present static society racked by rituals and medievalism must give way to a dynamic, forward-looking society with modern habits, values, and living (see chapter 9). A few examples would dramatically illustrate this national tendency, both amongst its leaders as well as its people, to wait for the riches to fall from heaven or to find undiscovered treasure troves. The present government announced to a deprived nation about the impending discovery of oil deposits in offshore Karachi larger than that of oil-rich Kuwait and said that soon all the economic woes would be over and that the nation would give money to other countries instead of begging for loans from other nations. Of course, there was no such oil discovery despite Prime Minister Khan's appeal to his people to pray to Allah by offering two *nafals salat*. Previous government of Nawaz

Sharif had also announced the discovery of nonexistent unlimited gold deposits in Panjab province, while one car mechanic announced to a stunned, euphoric nation his invention of a car engine running on water as fuel.

Karachi Calling

When we talk about development of Pakistan and uplifting it to the next level of nation-states, we should make a special mention of the importance of the economic resurrection of metropolitan Karachi, a city of 20 plus million souls. Karachi being the anchor city of Pakistan is not like any other city of the country; its premier status comparable to other reputable autonomous cities of Asian region, Hong Kong, Singapore, Seoul, Bangkok, Kuala Lumpur, Jakarta that lead their respective nations. For the growth and prosperity of Karachi and for the greater good of the country, Karachi too needs full autonomy, at least for self-administration if not political sovereignty.

The growth and development of this anchor city generally has a ripple effect on the development of the rest of the country. When the federal government in the '50s and '60s was making some investment on the city's infrastructure, it progressed rapidly, and so did the rest of the country follow in Karachi's footsteps. And when the investment on Karachi stopped, the progress of the whole country slowed down on cue. It is said that as Karachi goes, so does Pakistan. It is the hub and the pace setter of the country's commercial and industrial center.

If indeed the city of Karachi contributes about 60% of the country's revenues to the national kitty, then why can't it be allocated and allowed to spend a decent fraction of that revenue on the city's ruined roads, streets, transport, parks, schools, sewerage system, on cleaning up the mountains of garbage, on perennial shortages of electric, power and water supply, on lack of safety and security, on creating jobs,, and on building other essential infrastructure? It's a fair question indeed. In this modern world, it's hard to imagine a mega city of more than twenty million without a train metro system.

A modest, laid-back, coastal city of about three hundred thousand at the time of country's independence, Karachi, almost overnight, had to absorb and play host to millions of refugees streaming across India to its hospitable shores. As if that exodus wasn't enough, in subsequent years it had to accommodate a second wave of economic refugees from Pakistan's up-country regions, all of whom were looking for jobs and opportunity.

The tragedy of Karachi, as it now lies in near ruins, totally neglected, was that at the precise time when it was poised to take off, it was hit by a deluge of gun violence, drug cartels, land mafias, bloodthirsty terror groups, rampaging mullahs, and political exploiters of the city. It became a city under siege. The very occurrence of this cataclysmic disaster in an inherently peaceful, gentle, live-and-let-live city established a prima facie case of wanton, gross negligence on the part of the government.

If the governments of the day had not treated Karachi with such callousness, apathy, and criminal neglect, if they had invested a little in its infrastructure, security, and safety, if they had facilitated its growth and progress, if they had paid heed to the voices of citizens, Pakistan would have been a different kind of a country today. People are reminded of other great anchor and gateway cities of Asia, such as Hong Kong, Singapore, Bangkok, and Shanghai, all of which are beacons of prosperity and progress, and they ask, "Why not Karachi?"

Balochistan Impasse

This book would be incomplete if no mention is made of Balochistan and its simmering restlessness and uprising. Balochistan is of course Pakistan's largest province, comprising of about half the total land mass of the country, with a population of about 70 million people. It has a geostrategic location as its port city of Gwadar sits at the mouth of the Arab Gulf. Its rich in oil, gas and valuable minerals. Yet it is the least developed and poorest of the four provinces of the country in terms or per capita income.[8]

Historically speaking, Balochistan has existed as an independent princely state in the form of *Khanite* of Kalat under the rule of Khan of

Kalat long before Pakistan gained its freedom in 1947 and became an independent state. Its independent status was initially acknowledged by Pakistan's ruling party, the Pakistan Muslim League.[9] However, Pakistan in an apparent change of heart, in 1948 proposed to the Khan a merger with the newly formed state of Pakistan. How ironic that this proposal to merge was made by Pakistan's founder and its first Governor General, Mohammad Ali Jinnah, the same Mr. Jinnah who had represented Kalat before the British Privy Council to espouse the sovereignty and independence of Kalat and had argued against its annexation by Britain.

Khan of Kalat placed this Pakistan proposal to the state's assembly for vote. Both houses of the parliament decisively rejected this proposal and voted for an independent and sovereign Balochistan. [10] What followed after that was an ignoble chapter in Pakistan's history and the beginnings of bloodshed and endless conflicts.in that region.

Pakistan launched many military operations to quell this Balochistan insurgency. Army's biggest operation was the 5-year, 1973-1978 operation under Gen Tikka Khan that was initiated during Zulfiqar Ali Bhutto's rule when he dissolved the Balochistan Assembly. Heavy weapons and fighter planes were deployed, result in many casualties on both the sides. Eventually the uprising seemed to subside and in 1977 Lt Gen Rahim Uddin Khan offered a general amnesty to the insurgents. Another notable operation was ordered by Gen Parvaiz Musharraf that resulted in the death of Balochi prominent separatist leader, Sardar Akbar Bugti. on August 26, 2006.

The long insurgency and separatist movement in Balochistan now seem to have slowed down buy by no means it's over and died down. With allegations of enforced disappearance, killings and dumping of activists and civilians, stories of torture, jailing, and other human rights violations of citizens, the insurgency and the state actions to tackle it has not been great for the country's image and reputation. The movement is spearheaded by Balochistan National Front (BNF), Balochistan Liberation Army (BLA) and other splintered groups Its prominent leaders have been Akbar Bugti, Khair Baksh Mazari, Attaullah Mangal, Ghous Baksh Bizenjo and other younger tribal leaders. Human rights activists such as Mama Qadeer, Mehtab Baloch and many others have led Long Marches, protests to spotlight the plight and victimization of Baloch women, children and civilians.

Finding a solution for Balochistan that is long lasting and fair and beneficial to the people of the torn, volatile province is paramount for Pakistan. If it is weighed down by the Baloch unrest, it would be difficult for the country to achieve economic progress and social uplift all across the four provinces. The question remains as to what exactly would such a solution entail?

Its key components would have to a willingness for reconciliation and for giving Balochis a fair shake of the economic pie, especially the portion derived from the provinces own rich natural resources. Yes, the Pakistan Government has periodically made somewhat half-hearted, feeble attempts to pacify the Balochi nationalists by offering monetary packages to the province for its development but so far, all such attempts at reconciliations have not been a decisive success . It's about time the Federal Government displays maturity, sincerity of purpose, flexibility, and seriousness in acceding to the autonomy . governance, social and trading rights of the Balochi people.

CHAPTER 3

Introspection: Assault on the Constitution

Before moving forward, the nation requires a necessary introspection, an inquiry to Identify those who were responsible for trampling over the rule of law and the constitutional order in vogue for the nation to learn lessons from the past transgressions.

Here is the oath of the office of the chief justice, supreme, and high-court judges of Pakistan: *"I do solemnly swear that I will bear true faith and allegiance to Pakistan: That I will preserve, protect and defend the Constitution of the Islamic Republic of Pakistan."*

Here is the oath of the office of members of the armed forces of Pakistan: *"I do solemnly swear that I will bear true faith and allegiance to Pakistan and uphold the Constitution of the Islamic Republic of Pakistan which embodies the will of the people, that I will not engage myself in any political activities whatsoever."*

Once upon a time, a country was gifted to its future elites who were waiting in the wings like birds of prey to pounce and feast upon it without giving a hoot about the plight of its downtrodden people. The rest, as they say, is history.

The story of Pakistan is a story for preeminence and domination of the nation's milieu primarily by two actors, the judiciary and the military, in the name of rule of law and national interest. This is not to say that other predatory actors were not so inclined in the milieu, such as some politicians, feudal lords, mullahs, bureaucrats, and businessmen, and haven't had their share of power grabs and exploitation, but at the very top level of the food chain, the judiciary and military take the cake. [9]

This analysis should not be viewed as a wholesale, across-the-board condemnation of the personnel of these two elite institutions. In fact, both these institutions have produced some men of integrity, courage, honesty, and professionalism. Judges such as A. R Cornelius, M. R. Kalyani, and Qazi Faye Isa and generals such as Abdul Waheed Kakar, Jehangir Karamat, and Akhtar Hussain Malik shine bright on the firmament of these two institutions. Question as to why these two institutions should be lumped together may be answered by the fact that interventions, violations, and manipulations of the constitution and the rule of law in Pakistan have been so intertwined that it became increasingly difficult to separate the two when discussing the politics of the country. Therefore, it makes better sense to treat these twin threats and attacks on the country's legal structure in a joint fashion.

Judiciary and Military's Sad Role

While Pakistan's military establishment has brought about five coups and overthrows of the constitution, it has also creatively introduced and imposed on the country such extra constitutional machinations as martial laws, legal framework orders, provisional constitutional orders, basic democracy.[6] It directly ruled the country for no less than thirty-six years and indirectly controlled the body politic from behind the scene, calling the shots for about twenty more years in the nation's seventy-year history. On the other hand, the country's judiciary has been playing a supportive role in military's unconstitutional seizures of power by legitimizing coups and their variations on dubious, invalid and novel grounds.[10]

Art of the Coup

The military's most brazen, in-your-face violations of the constitution, of course, have been its executions of coup d'états and the overthrow of the prevailing constitution and seizure of civilian power.[8] This basically manifested itself in two forms. One was the typical, old-fashioned, traditional coup d'état, simply overthrowing the constitution and grabbing power, while the second was the more subtle, sophisticated kind of a coup—precursor of a coup without a coup, but no less lethal. This second category was perfected by General Musharraf, who called himself the "chief executive" and employed constitutional look-alike devices such as the provisional constitutional order (PCO) to perpetuate his military rule. [4]

Constitutional Manipulations

Though civilian politicians had a significant hand in delaying promulgation of a constitution and then manipulating the constitution that was supposed to be the supreme and controlling law of the land, the military rulers were the ones who spearheaded a frontal assault on it. First, they flouted the constitution by bringing about military coups and then introduced distorted versions of it to suit their dictatorial whims. After discarding the 1956 constitution, which was then in vogue, General Ayyub Khan replaced it with his novel 1962 constitution, which held its presidential system and basic democracy as its centerpiece. [1]

The biggest damage to constitutional rule in Pakistan was done by General Zia ul Haq, who publicly said that the constitution was "just a piece of paper" that he could shred to pieces. And he did. He introduced a mangled, Islamized version of the 1973 constitution that was full of anomalies and contradictions as seen in the next section, and the nation continues to pay a heavy price for it. He also inserted in the constitution a new provision, specifically Article 58-2(b), which gave him as president absolute power to dismiss the national assembly and the prime minister. This provision was later repealed by the civilian government via the !8th Amendment to the Constitution.

Constitutional Anomalies

As a result of General Zia's manipulations, the present version of the 1973 Pakistan Constitution is a tortured hodgepodge of documents. Its lofty democratic rhetoric time and again is shot down by frenzied sentiments of faith. In his Islamist zeal, General Zia unilaterally and unlawfully incorporated inconsistent and improper provisions in the constitution. For instance, Article 25(1) of the constitution states, "All citizens are equal before law and are entitled to equal protection of law." Equality of citizens and "equal protection of law" have come to universally mean absolutely no discrimination by the state on the basis of a citizen's religion and religious beliefs, color of skin, ethnic origin, race, or gender.

And yet the constitution expressly bars non- Muslim minorities from being appointed either as the prime minister or the president of the country, Article 41(2) provides, "A person shall not be qualified for election as President unless he is a Muslim.", while Article 91(3) states, "The National Assembly ... must elect one of its MUSLIM members to be ... the Prime Minister." [3] As is obvious, this is an open and brazen denial of a citizen's equal rights along the lines of religious apartheid. . Similarly, Article 260, that does define who a "Muslim" is, effectively excludes some unorthodox sects, like the Ahmedis from being considered as "Muslims" as per the constitution.

In another ambiguity, Article 62(1)(d), which disqualifies from membership of the national assembly a person if he or she "violates Islamic Injunctions." The term "Islamic Injunctions" is not defined in the constitution and is left to another body, the Council of Islamic Ideology to define it later.

Moreover, General Zia included in the constitution the controversial, destabilizing, overly broad, and ambiguous Article 62(1)(f), which requires an assembly member to be "sagacious, righteous and non-profligate, honest and Ameen" to qualify, and Article 184(3), which bestows an unfettered jurisdiction to the supreme courts regarding enforcement of fundamental rights in matters of "high public importance." This provision was subsequently used by the judiciary to disqualify an elected, lawful prime minster for life. See Chief Justice Saqib Nisar in one of the following sections.

Judiciary's Complicity

In third world countries, the military with its propensity for grabbing power tends to seek alliances of convenience with judiciary.[2] But in the case of Pakistan, the judiciary's acquiescence and collaboration exceeded the expectations of the military. Not only did the judiciary remove no less than three elected heads of governments who were becoming irritants for the military, but it also provided legitimacy to army coups, condoned overthrows of the constitution and rule of law, and even banned an elected prime minster for life from political elections. The road to Pakistan military's domination in politics was thus made as smooth as the prime minister Nawaz Sharif's Islamabad-Lahore Motorway.[14]

While the military's role in assaulting the constitution was pretty straightforward with the usage of the old-fashioned coup to trash the constitutional order, remove the civilian government of the day, and grab political power, the judiciary's role in such actions was nuanced and dressed in legal language, coopting the fictitious "doctrine of society" as a springboard to support the coups and later abuses of special or *suo moto* jurisdiction granted to the Supreme Court under Article 184(3) of the constitution to hound the democratically elected civilian rulers.[7][12]

Doctrine of Necessity

Tamizuddin Khan Case

In the year 1955, when the sights and sounds of the mighty British Empire were still fresh in the minds of the people of the newly created state, the then chief justice of the Pakistan Supreme Court, Justice Mohammad Munir, was so much in awe of the British laws that he would rather protect the Queen's representative, Governor General Ghulam Mohammad, than the assembly of the new independent state. [13] Yes, we are talking about the Maulvi Tamizuddin Khan case made famous by the infamous "doctrine of necessity" in the country's political history. Ghulam Mohammad unceremoniously dissolved the constituent assembly along with dismissal of the assembly's speaker, Maulvi Tamizuddin Khan, who initially petitioned and won in the Sindh High Court against his unlawful dismissal on flimsy grounds.[5] In the eyes of Ghulam Mohammad, the assembly's fault was its enacting an amendment to the Government of India Act of 1935 that divested him of the authority to dismiss the cabinet ministers of the government.

The 1947 India Independence Act, passed by the British parliament, under which the partition of the subcontinent took place, gave no such dismissal powers to the governor general. Justice Munir incredibly supported the dissolution of the assembly, invoking an ancient British relic of its common law, Brocton's maxim, which indicated "that which is otherwise not legal is made lawful by necessity." It was a facetious application of this so-called doctrine of necessity, which was meant for private individual's unlawful acts and not a doctrine to be applicable in political domains as is evident by the fact that no other democratic country has any precedent of its usage in constitutional litigations.

Moreover, Justice Munir, the legal genius, failed to notice the irony in upholding the parliamentary supremacy on the one hand (British parliament's Indian Independence Act) while refusing to protect the same in the dissolution of Pakistan's parliament on the other hand.

If laws of colonial England were still applicable in an independent Pakistan because it was a *dominion*, then what was the point of giving independence and freedom to this new nation? As constitutional historian Hamid Khan puts it, "It was Justice Munir's duty to apply the law and to decide correctly regardless of consequences. The issuance of writ (order) was his province and not its enforcement." One justification Munir gave for supporting the dissolution of the assembly was that its continuance might result in disorder, even though he knew, as did the governor general, that the constituent assembly was on the verge of presenting the country's first constitution to the nation.

General Ayub's Coup

The most damaging ramification arising out of this ill-thought, fatal, wrong decision was that it paved the way for the future judiciary to defend the overthrow of the constitution and rule of law by military coups. And sure enough, soon thereafter, the army chief General Mohammad Ayub Khan, salivating in the wings for power, executed a military coup on October 7, 1958, toppling the civil government and the president of Pakistan, Iskandar Mirza, overthrowing the 1956 Constitution of Pakistan, installing himself first as the chief martial law administrator and then as the president of the country. [11] As if on cue, the Supreme Court validated Ayub's illegal coup on October 27, 1958, and his martial regime through its ruling in the Dosso legal case (PLD 1958 SC 553) on the basis of the previously outlined doctrine of necessity and Kallsen's left-wing theory that revolutions are a legitimate means of changing the government.

Emboldened by the judiciary's abdication of its duty to defend the constitution and its support of his dictatorship, General Ayub Khan took no time in imposing his own constitutional version, specifically the 1962 constitution, on a hapless nation that contained his presidential system of government and an election system of basic democracy to perpetuate his own dictatorial rule. Just as before, the judiciary was missing in action and did not stand up to a usurper of rule of law.

General Yahya's Martial Law

In the face of countrywide protests against his rule, General Ayub Khan relinquished power in 1969, and on March 25, 1969, he appointed army chief General Yahya Khan as the next president of Pakistan. Khan immediately instituted martial law in the country without the judiciary challenging this unconstitutional step. To his credit, General Yahya held the country's fair general elections, and these saw the emergence of East Pakistani leader Sheikh Mujib – ur- Rehman and his political party, the Awami League, as winners. However, General Yahya's delay in transferring power to Rehman ignited the separatist rebellion of

East Pakistani Bengalis because of perceived domination of West Pakistan. General Yahya's order for the army to ruthlessly suppress the Bengalis resulted in atrocities and in a humiliating and massive defeat at the hands of the Indian Army and the eventual cessation of East Pakistan and the establishment of an independent state of Bangladesh therein. Yahya resigned on December 20, 1970, but his short-lived, extraconstitutional rule proved to be most catastrophic for Pakistan.

General Zia's Coup

By now the judiciary's silence and unwillingness to challenge the overthrow of democratic rule was fairly established, and the generals learned their lesson well. They could now count on the tacit support of the judiciary in their unlawful power grabbing anytime they chose to do so. However, the 1971 war in East Pakistan and the army's surrender and consequent separation of the country's eastern wing perhaps precluded the military from seizing power sooner. As such, on July, 1977, General Zia- ul- Haq, the army chief (COAS) on the grounds of rigged elections, launched Operation Fair Play to dispose of the democratic head of government, specifically the brilliant and charismatic Zu Ali Bhutto. General Zia -ul- Haq declared martial law and overthrew the consensus 1973 Constitution of Pakistan. The Supreme Court, headed by Chief Justice Anwar ul Haq, upheld General Zia's coup, his implementation of martial law, and his overthrow of the Pak Constitution on the basis of now familiar legalization tool of the doctrine of necessity (see the Nusrat Bhutto case). [15]

In all fairness to the judiciary, the wily and cunning General Zia- ul- Haq diluted the powers of the superior judiciary by establishing military courts under his martial law regulations and the *Shariat* Court for enforcing Islamic injunctions. He also divided the powerful Lahore High Court into smaller courts at various locations of Panjab province. However, the question remains: Why didn't the Supreme Court hold him accountable when he failed to conduct new elections within ninety days as he had promised the nation?

General Musharraf's Coup

General Musharraf's coup and seizure of Nawaz Sharif's elected civil government on October 12, 1999, was the stuff of cheap B-rated action movies. Prime Minister Nawaz Sharif fired General Musharraf as a consequence of Musharraf's *Kargil* debacle (when Musharraf executed an ill-thought-out, ill-planned, foolish operation against the Indian forces crossing the internationally agreed-on line of control [LOC] in the Indian-held Kashmir territory), which could have triggered an all-out war with India but for the timely intervention of US President Clinton. It turned out that at the time when Nawaz Sharif issued orders of Musharraf's dismissal, the latter was on board a plane bringing him back home from a visit to Sri Lanka. When Musharraf got news of his firing, he immediately contacted the army's GHQ via the plane's communications system and garnered support from the military. With plane's fuel running dangerously low, he ordered the arrest of Prime Minister Sharif on grounds of hijacking the plane, incredulous as that seemed.

During the next few years, the country witnessed an intricate cat-and-mouse game between the fired army chief and the democratic head of the government. General Musharraf was a man driven by blind ambition and lust for power. Nothing could stop him then—neither the Pakistan Constitution nor a few old civilians sitting on the Supreme Court. He mocked the constitution and circumvented it novel ways in vainglorious attempts to absolve himself of treason in the overthrow of the constitution and the lawful government of Mr. Nawaz Sharif.

First, he declared himself as the chief executive of the country rather than the head of the state, a designation he subsequently changed to become the president of Pakistan.[16] Two days after the coup, he declared a national emergency, and on January 20, 2000, he imposed the Provisional Constitutional Order (PCO) to replace the country's existing 1973 constitution. Chief Justice Salimuzzaman Siddiqui of the country's Supreme Court legalized this coup and overthrow of the constitution for a period of three years maximum under the "doctrine of necessity" basis cited by the court in defense of previous coups.

However, Justice Siddiqui later had a change of heart and ruled that Musharraf's coup was a "violation of the constitution." After this change of heart, General Musharraf promptly dismissed and replaced him. On May 12, 2000, the new chief justice, Irshad Hasan, then validated this coup by virtue of the doctrine of necessity but ordered Musharraf to hold the general elections. Subsequently, on April 30, 2002, to satisfy the judiciary, General Musharraf did hold a fake referendum to validate his illegal rule for five years.

In his insatiable quest for power, perhaps General Musharraf was the lone military dictator who had the dubious distinction of bringing about a second coup during his tenure. This he accomplished by imposing a second martial law and suspending the then Chief Justice Choudhary Iftikhar Uddin upon his refusal to take oath of office under the PCO, even though the 1873 constitution was restored. This action triggered massive protests and a long march by the country's lawyers and members of the civil society. This Lawyers Movement was successful in forcing Musharraf to reinstate Chief Justice Iftikhar Uddin, and eventually, he had to give up power and order general elections under a caretaker government.

Judicial Tyranny

Chaudhary Iftikhar

Ironically, the advent of Chief Justice Choudhary Iftikhar on Pakistan's Supreme Court did not usher in a democratic era for the nation, even though he was reinstated into office on the heels of popular nationwide protests for the restoration of democracy and independence of the judiciary (led by lawyers within the Lawyers Movement). On March 9, 2007, former president General Musharraf had declared Iftikhar to be a "nonfunctional chief justice" because of his refusal to legalize Musharraf's continued rule. After the above Lawyers Movement, on July 20, 2007, in a much-awaited landmark verdict, the Supreme Court reinstated Iftikhar as the chief justice and threw out some misconduct references against him. Unfortunately, instead of a judicial reawakening,

Iftikhar's vindication heralded the advent of a judicial tyranny of *suo moto* that would not only trample the constitutional order but also create political uncertainty and economic misery across the land.

Like a carnivorous animal that cannot change its man-hunting ways once it gets a taste of human flesh, a human being who gets the taste of power will similarly not let go of it easily. Chief Justice Iftikhar's judiciary was a case in point. How else can one explain the actions of the Supreme Court during Iftikhar's reign from 2007 to 2013 that took *"suo moto notices"* of such purely administrative matters as GST tax, the pricing of petrol, even the price of 'samosas', for heaven's sake, and overturned the government's appointments of civil servants like the chief of Pakistan International Airlines (PIA).

As everyone knew, Pakistan's whole justice system from the lowest *kutchery* courts upward was a cesspool of corruption and inefficiency with a black hole of pending cases. Yet its apex judiciary, abdicating its own duty to put its own house in order, rushed helter-skelter to take notice of the GST tax imposed by the elected executive government as if it was in a contest with the government for control of executive power.

People had a right to ask exactly what all this judicial overreach and arbitrariness and all the Supreme Court notices and orders had actually achieved for the country's masses. Did judiciary's activism make any difference in the lives of the ordinary people? Did such actions economically benefit the people? Did they make the country safer and more stable? Did they make the availability of essential commodities, electricity, and other basic items easier and less expensive? Did the overall economy of the country improve? Did the chaotic, terror-ridden security situation in Balochistan and Karachi improved after its suo moto intervention pursuant to Article 184(3) of the Constitution.

Of course, the answer will be in the negative on all counts. On the other hand, the situation on the ground undeniably further deteriorated in all of the previously outlined areas where the Supreme Court had intervened. The judiciary of Choudhary Iftikhar wasted the country's precious time and limited resources on a myriad of frivolous, nonproductive *suo moto* notices, hearings, inquiries, and petitions such as the *Memogate* or the National Reconciliation Ordinance (NRO) case. Recall how CJ Iftikhar in his pursuit of the NRO case put the government's stability and the state's viability at grave political risk by coercing the Prime Minister to write a letter to Swiss authorities to reopen investigation against the President of Pakistan even though the latter enjoyed complete immunity under the Pakistan Constitution.

CJ Iftikhar's role in domestic commercial cases such as stopping the privatization of Pakistan Steel Mills (PSM), Pakistan International Airlines (PIA) and other state-owned enterprises amounted to unwanted and improper interference in the economic affairs of the country that resulted in enormous losses. His penchant for interference in international contracts, containing binding arbitration clauses, such as the *Reko Diq*, TCC and Turkish Powerboat rental cases, was deem able as tortuous interference that ultimately triggered multi-billion-dollar arbitration judgements against our cash-deprived nation. In the process the rule of law and the bedrock principle of separation of powers of the three branches of the government, which is embedded in our constitution, were dealt a severe blow. Many of the country's key institutions such as the police, Federal Investigative Agency (FIA), National Accountability Bureau (NAB), Oil & Gas Regulatory Authority (OGRA), and other law-enforcement agencies and institutions, were undermined.

Terrorists had been let loose and unleashed murder and mayhem in the land, and the country's security situation worsened as a result of the judiciary's interference in governance. To stifle the voice of the people, to silence any criticism in the media, and to preempt any public debate or discussion over the excesses committed by it, the judiciary wrongly used the "contempt of court" powers under Article 204(2)(b) of the Constitution of Pakistan to silence all who dare question it. In no other democratic country in the world would a court of law be allowed to abuse its contempt powers by applying them outside the court's premises in order to abridge that most fundamental of human rights, the right to free speech and expression.

And as the citizens had by now come to shockingly realize, through the ad nauseum invoking of the controversial *suo moto* Article 184(c)(3) of the Constitution, the apex court had been ruling on any matter under the sun at its pleasure—policies ranging from the price of samosas to the price of CNG and electricity, from the transfer of civil servants to the removal of an elected head of the government, all under the pretext of "enforcement of fundamental rights" or a "matter of public importance."

Such sweeping, antidemocratic articles were surreptitiously and spuriously inserted in the constitution to be subsequently used as authoritarian tools or ploys by the courts for the sole purpose of suppressing the elected representatives and will of the people. Perhaps not content with its relentless intrusions and the marauding of the previously weak, submissive, and inept government, it seemed apparent that this judiciary was now eyeing the new Pakistan Muslim League-Nawaz (PMLN) government as its prey.

Prime Minister Nawaz Sharif and his PMLN government's carelessness in misjudging the imperial ambitions of the judiciary and failure to nip this judicial hazard in the bud foreordained that his government would meet the same fate as did the previous government of Pakistan People's Party (PPP) and Yousuf Raza Gilani. With its fire stoked by a pliant and self-serving media and vested, parsimonious interests of the security establishment, this judiciary wasn't prone to stop lording over the elected government and the people's parliament on its own volition.

Arsalan's Case

In June 2012, former chief justice Choudhary Iftikhar, misusing 'suo moto' powers, assumed the hearing of a graft case against his son Arsalan, which involved alleged bribery paid by a big developer named Malik Riaz, in order to preempt adjudication of these charges in another court. Very conveniently, the Supreme Court bench then issued a short order absolving Iftikhar of such judicial abuse and prematurely ordered the hearing of his son's case without any investigation or examination of any evidence in the underlying imbroglio. The proprietary of this Supreme Court action was in fact contradicted by the Supreme Court's own statement in that order, which stated, "The Supreme Court ...

cannot judge the guilt or innocence of the parties without evidence or trial." So how was this ruling not applicable to the chief justice who was so intertwined in this scandal? He was the father of one of the main suspects, and his judicial power was at the heart of this corruption scandal.

This did not imply that Arsalan was himself guilty, but there couldn't be any exemption from inquiry and investigation along with other participants and witnesses for possible criminal violations based just on mere words of one of the parties. Who was Malik Riaz to give a clean bill of health to the chief justice? It was strange that the Supreme Court was relying on the good word of Malik Riaz, a businessman whom the former once considered to be an accused fit to be prosecuted for some serious criminal offenses under Pakistan's criminal laws.

To contend that the media was maligning the judiciary by highlighting this scandal was to blame the messenger and not the message. In this connection corruption in the media, which no doubt prevailed was a convenient distraction, and was less important than the imperative of our judiciary to have an unassailable reputation and an image above reproach. Conducting a thorough probe or inquiry of all those allegedly involved, including CJ Iftikhar would have cleared rather than tarnished the judiciary's reputation and removed the dark clouds hanging over the country's most esteemed institution.

The nation had a right to know answers to such vital questions as how long Iftikhar knew about his son's involvement with Malik Riaz and how many meetings the then chief justice had with Malik Riaz before the matter was seized through a *suo moto* action. The only other acceptable alternative to such an inquiry would have been for the chief justice to have quit honorably in the larger interests of the judiciary and the country. But this was not to be.

It appeared that the rule of law in our land had been supplanted by a rule, by a surfeit of *suo moto* suits. Although in the suo moto matter of the chief justice's son and Malik Riaz, it was a case of one suo moto too many—the one that backfired and the one that might come to haunt the judiciary for years to come.

Whether dwelling on issues of purely executive governance (sugar pricing, highway bypasses, bureaucratic postings and transfers, etc.) or of the separation of legislative powers (speaker's parliamentary rulings, disqualification of assembly members, etc.) or of the admissions and adjudication of petitions (lack of legal standing and subject-matter jurisdiction in the memo case, usurpation of powers of the executive branch in the contempt case, etc.), the misuse of the original jurisdiction by the judiciary has been whimsical and arbitrary.

Far from strengthening the rule of law in our country, this judicial adventurism under the cover of Article 184(3) *suo moto* jurisdiction created a climate of political instability in the country. It undermined the law-enforcing and prosecutorial institutions, increased the cost of doing business with Pakistan by millions of dollars, and above all, diverted the judiciary from performing its basic constitutional function of deciding thousands of regular cases that are languishing before the apex court on appeal. It is about time the nation discarded the anomalous, overreaching Article 184(3) in the dustbin of history and thus join the other democratic nations of the world in matters of judicial oversight.

Our knee-jerk reaction to this alleged corruption and blackmail scandal the moment it unfolded in the media seems to indicate the prevalence of a national psychosis or a mind-set of paranoia, delusion, and denial—ones that are reminiscent of the lugubrious, conspiratorial days of the 9/11 terror attack and the May 2 raid and killing of Osama bin Laden.. It seems that whenever some of our preconceived myths or assumptions are shattered by a stark, unyielding, and yet truthful reality, we tend to revert to denial and a refusal to face up to the facts as they are. In the case of the 9/11 attacks, our long-held assumptions that all Muslims believers adhere to the peaceful precepts of Islam was shattered and laid bare. As we all know, our preferred mode of coping with these setbacks was to spin a web of conspiracy theories.

If the current national gridlock does bring down the edifice of democracy once again, it would be the fault of our three institutions— the army because of its running the country's foreign and security policy; the government because of its inept, nontransparent, and ineffective performance; and the judiciary because of its support of extra-constitutional measures, overarching adjudication and creation of roadblocks in political governance.

Concerning our superior judiciary, we have created and embedded in our minds an illusion of an incorruptible judiciary that is beyond mendacious politics, mundane temptation, and inveterate ambition. As soon as this high-flying myth came crashing down to reality with this corruption case, we reacted with conspiracy theories, of course. Until we stop believing in fairy tales and the last bastions of hope that Ayyub will save us, that Zia will save us, that Bhutto will save us, that the army will save us, and now that the judiciary will save us, we will continue to be hugely disappointed and doomed to live perennially in these parlous times with one setback after another.

Removal of Prime Minister

In February of 2012, Chaudhary Iftikhar's Supreme Court indicted the then prime minister (PM) Yusuf Raza Gilani for contempt of court for his refusal to send a letter to Swiss authorities to reopen a graft case against President Asif Ali Zardari. Gilani rightly argued that any pursuit of a possible criminal offense against the Zardari was a moot point since Zardari as president enjoyed full immunity while in office from prosecution under the Pakistan Constitution. In April 2012, Iftikhar, in a milestone verdict, convicted PM Gilani on contempt charges of "ridiculing the judiciary" by his refusal to follow up the alleged graft case against President Zardari.

Apart from other questionable conclusions drawn by the learned justices, a review of the judgment reveals a stunning ruling—the misuse and misapplication of a defunct and extinct law (the expired Contempt of Court Ordinance V of 2003) to convict and punish the constitutional and democratically elected prime minister who was not a party in litigation in the underlying case of *Dr. Mubashir Hassan v. Federation of Pakistan*. In paragraph 68, page 65 of the judgment, the honorable court states, "The said Ordinance V of 2003 derives its authority from Article 204 (3) of the Constitution, Article 204 (2) of the Constitution empowers this Court to punish a person for committing 'Contempt of Court.'"

First, assuming that the old 2003 contempt ordinance "derived its authority" from Article 204(3) of the constitution, the central issue was not the constitutional authority of the said ordinance but whether this ordinance had current validity because of the time sensitivity and temporary nature of the ordinance.

The fact is that all ordinances, including the obsolete 2003 Contempt of Court Ordinance, unlike regular laws or acts enacted by the legislature, are unique, ad hoc, stop-gap measures or what are called "sunset laws" having a fixed, limited, and specified duration. They are creatures of the Pakistan Constitution, specifically and solely Article 89 of the constitution, which exclusively empowers the president to promulgate an ordinance only for a short, limited time in order to deal with an urgent situation, namely when parliament is not in session and when "circumstances exist, which render it necessary to take immediate (legal) action" (Article 89).

When it comes to defining the parameters of an ordinance, Article 89 of our constitution and not Article 204 is the controlling and governing law. It is aptly titled "Power of President to Promulgate Ordinances." Clause 1 and 2 of Article 89 details the time duration (120 days), extension (only one permitted), repeal, expiration, and its possible enactment by parliament. Moreover, the preamble of the 2003 Contempt of Court Ordinance expressly specifies the source of its power or authority, "In exercise of the powers conferred by clause (1) of Article 89 of the Constitution ... the President is pleased to make and promulgate the ... Ordinance."

Second, upon resurrection and misapplication of this ineffective and defunct law (2003 Ordinance) to convict the PM, the Iftikhar's Supreme Court in paragraph 68, page 65 of the judgment improperly states that "Article 204 (2) of the Contempt Ordinance empowers this Court to punish a person for committing Contempt of Court." Like other ordinances, this one had expired a long time ago. The 2003 Ordinance was promulgated in about July of 2003 for a temporary period of 120 days pursuant to Article 89 of the constitution. Perhaps it got one extension for an additional period of 120 days after that.

The fact is that this ordinance was never laid before parliament as a bill and converted into or adopted by parliament as a regular statutory law or an act, which was clearly required by Article 89(2). Consequently, the ordinance expired, lapsed, and became obsolete or nonexistent as a prevailing and effective law of the land.

It is a well-established principle of law that courts do not interpret, effectuate, adjudicate, or take into consideration a law that has expired or lapsed, no matter how exiguous the offense is. Once a law lapses because of its limited time frame or because of inherent sunset provisions, it loses its effectiveness and validity. An extinct law cannot also be applied prospectively. Thus, the Supreme Court cannot use or apply this expired 2003 Contempt Ordinance to punish the prime minister since this ordinance is not in vogue or in force and is not a prevailing or enforceable law of the land. Article 204(3) of the constitution, regardless of any derived authority, cannot resurrect a dead ordinance such as the 2003 Contempt Ordinance.

Third, in arbitrarily dismissing the attorney general's sound argument that no law of contempt was in force in the country since the Contempt Ordinance of 2003 lapsed under Article 89, the honorable court in paragraph 47, page 44 of the judgment summarily and arbitrarily dismissed this correct contention by citing an old 2007 case (Suo Moto Case No. 1 of 2007), where the Supreme Court held this ordinance to be valid and prevailing. However, that case and the Justice Hasnat Ahmed Khan case was not relevant and could not have been used as persuasive precedents because, as pointed out previously, the subject ordinance was time-sensitive with its sunset restriction.

Unlike parliamentary acts, the ordinance came with an expiration date. Therefore, even assuming that it was valid and in force in 2007, it couldn't be so in the year 2012 after a further lapse of five years. Moreover, those two cases were vastly distinguishable in nature of circumstances and controversy from the matter at hand.

Fourth, the court in paragraph 47, page 44 erroneously asserted that "even if there was no sub-constitutional legislation (the Contempt Ordinance, 2003) regulating proceedings of Contempt of Court, the Court was possessed of constitutional power under Article 204 to punish the PM." This may or may not be true. However, this was purely an academic and moot point since the Supreme Court did choose to invoke this obsolete contempt ordinance and not Article 204 to sentence the prime minister. Furthermore, the said Article 204 clearly contemplates and mandates "the exercise" of contempt powers conferred on the court to "be regulated by law."

Fifth, the Supreme Court in its judgments went a long way in emphasizing its constitutional right of interpretation of law. No one can argue with this basic right of the Supreme Court. However, to the extent the application of the 2003 Contempt Ordinance is concerned, it is not a question of interpretation of its provisions. We are not discussing or interpreting the contents of this law. Simply put, this law expired a long time ago. It was no longer a prevailing law. Legally, it did not exist in the statute books. It ceased to be a law some time ago, so the question of its interpretation did not arise at all.

Sixth, this judgment holding the prime minister Gilani guilty of contempt violates some of the fundamental and constitutionally guaranteed principles of fair trial and due process, such as a right to a jury trial and the assumption of innocence during the trial among others. Paragraph 27 of the verdict reveals that the justices had already formed an opinion of guilt of the prime minister even before the arguments and trial began. A trial is adversarial in nature. It is one party (the prosecutor or the state) versus an individual defendant, the duty of the former being to prove and convince the judge of the culpability of the latter. In this case the prosecutor himself said that there was no evidence sufficient to establish the charges against the prime minister. So why, despite this assertion by the prosecutor, did the honorable court find the prime minister guilty of contempt charges? In addition, there was no jury in the trial as required by the constitution.

The impropriety of an extrajudicial note by Justice Khosa is worth mentioning. The learned judge referred to "the power of the people" and "Arab Spring." Inciting people to rebellion, to take the law in their own hands by coming out on the streets to subvert or overthrow a constitutionally established, elected government is very close to being treasonous under the constitution.

In general, people have a tendency to be complacent, to roll with the punches as they say in order to get by and get along. Well, this is almost always until the stark reality hits them in the face. It seems this was the case with the people taking the restraint, objectivity, and balance of our judiciary for granted until the Supreme Court's order to schedule the presidential elections and the accusation against Imran Khan of contempt of court woke them from their slumber.

Judicial Overreach

Unfortunately, the Pakistani Constitution is a badly drafted document that contains anomalies, contradictions, and obsolete, antiquated laws not found in other constitutions of the world. Two examples of two such antiquated laws are the notorious *suo moto* (Article 184(c)(3) and the contempt of court law (Article 204 (2)(b)) Articles, which are the source of the present judicial overreach.

The origins of the decadent and obsolete "contempt of court" law as it is written in our constitution—a law that prohibits ridiculing or criticizing the judiciary—dates back to colonial days when the British rulers of their colonies, for the sake of consolidation of their empire, thought fit to ban the natives from making fun of their kangaroo courts. Ever since the beginning of the modern era with its cardinal principle of the rule of law, freedom of speech has become the most cherished and undisputed right of the people. In the words of Justice Brennan of the US Supreme Court in the landmark case about freedom of speech (*The New York Times v. Sullivan*), "It is a prized privilege to speak one's mind, although not always in good taste, on all public institutions." That includes the judiciary. To suggest that a court in this modern, democratic day and age would use its contempt power to muffle the mouths of free citizens who choose to criticize the judges outside the court is simply preposterous. The judges are supposed to protect and not prevent free speech.

Nowadays when the matter of contempt of court comes up in a democratic country, it is either in the context of a judge invoking his or her contempt powers to punish a principled journalist or a stubborn witness in the courtroom for not disclosing the source of reporting or testimony. Or it is a judge using contempt to discipline the errant behavior of a litigant or other person in the courtroom in order to maintain the decorum or dignity of the court proceedings. Or it is used to hold in contempt one of the actual parties in a case for not abiding by the court's decision. Other than these three narrow, specific situations, the contempt powers are never used by the judiciary to violate or abridge the all-important freedom of speech guaranteed by our constitution through censoring criticism of the judiciary outside the four walls of the courtroom.

Moreover, something must be said about the equally antiquated law of suo moto jurisdiction of Article 184(c)(3) of our constitution, another relic of the fossilized British Empire. There is no question that the judiciary has employed this law as a one-size-fits-all tool to interfere, subvert, and usurp the functions of the executive and legislative branches of our system of government on the pretext of "matters of public importance."

Exploiting the special jurisdiction conferred upon SC for fundamental rights on matters of public importance under Article 184(3) of the Constitution, Nisar used it to extend his judicial powers into the realm of the executive branch. From fixing the price of petrol to transferring civil servants to disqualifying a democratically elected prime ministers- nothing was deemed beyond his cope or purview. Saqib Nisar had become the country's de facto Chief Executive, President, and Speaker of National Assembly. Accountable to no one, he lorded over Federal Investigation Authority (FIA), Pakistan International Airlines (PIA), National Accountability Bureau (NAB), Pakistan Electronic Regulatory Authority (PEMRA) and other institutions of the country.

Because of the reasons highlighted previously, these twin mordacious provisions of Pakistan's Constitution, specifically Article 184 (c) and Article 204(2)(b), which irresponsibly and indulgently bestow such illimitable powers to the country's judiciary, must be immediately scrapped and discarded in the dustbin of history. Of course, the repeal of these suo moto and contempt laws in itself may not usher in a trustworthy, efficient, clean, and responsive system of justice without requiring judges of unassailable integrity, indubitable honesty, acknowledged legal scholarship, and sound mind. However, we have to start somewhere, and such an intrepid action seems to be a good place to start.

Memogate Drama

A frivolous and politically motivated petition filed before the Supreme Court by a petitioner having no legal standing alleged that the then Pakistani ambassador to the United States, Hussain Haqqani, wrote a memorandum to the Admiral John Mullen, joint chief of staff of US Armed Forces, seeking his help in persuading the Obama administration to avert a feared takeover by Pakistan military of the country's elected, civil government. The memo was allegedly delivered to Admiral Mullen by Haqqani's friend Mansur Ijaz, a US businessman of Pakistani origin. Chief Justice Iftikhar Uddin admitted this petition for hearing, even though the petitioners had no legal standing pursuant to suo moto jurisdiction under Article 184(3) of Pakistan Constitution. Ambassador Haqqani was summoned back to Pakistan to face charges of treason. In the upshot, after eight years of proceedings, on February 14, 2019, the Supreme Court finally decided to wrap up this case as the petitioners failed to appear before the court.

In the controversial *Memogate* case, Chief Justice Iftikhar invoked the Supreme Court's original and special suo moto jurisdiction pursuant to Article 184(3) of the constitution and admitted Nawaz Sharif's petition on the ground of ensuring the enforcement of the petitioner's fundamental rights specified in Articles 9, 14 and 19-A.

This special jurisdiction is conditional and limited on account of practical necessity—lest the apex court is inundated with an endless plethora of petitions, for which it would have neither the time nor the resources to adjudicate. The petitioner was required to establish by persuasive evidence that the said memo had resulted in, or would irreparably result in a direct, actual, substantial violation of his fundamental rights as mentioned previously and to show that the remedy he seeks (i.e., an investigation or inquiry) would actually redress the actual harm or injury done to him. It was very doubtful that the petition would have overcome such a burden of proof in the hearing.

It was difficult to see how this memo directly and individually affected or impinged on the petitioner's fundamental rights under Article 9, which says, "No person shall be deprived of life and liberty,") and/or under Article 14, which pertains to "dignity of man," "privacy of home," and "torture for the purpose of extracting evidence."

Finally, the fundamental right pursuant to Article 19-A is the "right to have access to information in all matters of public information subject to regulations and reasonable restrictions imposed by all." This article was enacted through the Eighteenth Amendment to provide citizens access to official information that is already in government files. In this case the government was denying the very existence or possession of such information, and the petitioner had shown no such proof other than to ask the court to order an investigation into the possibility of the government's connection to the memo.

Moreover, mere speculation or the possibility of existence of any information in government hands was not enough to invoke the special jurisdiction of the court. The Supreme Court was required to adjudicate only those cases or petitions where the injury or harm to a citizen arising from infringement of his or her constitutionally-guaranteed fundamental rights is concrete and actual, not potential or abstract, where it is individual and personal and not general and vague.

Did the writing of this letter or memo by a foreign citizen or its submission to a US general resulted in any personal, direct, actual, or concrete violation or denial of his previously specified fundamental rights? If not, then clearly the petitioners failed to establish through pertinent evidence that they had such required legal standing to solicit this special jurisdiction of the court.

The case seemed to be inconsistent with the established principle of judicial review that the courts are prohibited from admitting or hearing cases that involve mainly political questions. There could be no doubt that the subject matter of the memo dealt with political issues and goals, namely the ways of preventing the army from averting a coup, of overthrowing of a civilian democratic government, and of strengthening of the executive branch. These were all issues that were non justiciable since they fell in the political domain and required political resolutions.

Nisar's Suo Moto Plus

Not to be outdone by Chief Justice Iftikhar's judicial excesses, Chief Justice Nisar, in pursuit of his own ambitions of becoming the ultimate savior judge of Pakistan who was worshipped by the people, embarked on a journey of judicial flight, escaping the bounds of the constitutional limits—damn the overriding principle of the separation of the three branches of the government enshrined in the constitution, damn the prohibited interference in executive matters, damn the oath to defend and respect the Constitution of Pakistan.

Nisar was on a power mission that seemed unstoppable to him, especially with the tacit backing of the military, which had a stake in the removal of the ruling, antiterrorism, and pro-peace Nawaz Sharif. According to his spurious misinterpretation of the *suo moto* jurisdiction of Article 184(3), CJ Nisar authorized the Supreme Court to rule on anything that involved "fundamental rights of public importance." Consequently, he could build dams because the right to water was a fundamental right of the citizens. He could manage hospitals because the right to life was a fundamental right. He could administer colleges and schools because education was a fundamental right and so forth. Chief Justice Choudhary Iftikhar was the violator of the Constitution of Pakistan, but Chief Justice Saqib Nisar was the hammer of Thor of the Pakistan Constitution, hammering it down to an unrecognizable shape. Nisar's legacy of judicial adventurism starts from the trilogy of *Panama* cases.

Panama Papers Case

After failing to dislodge the elected prime minister Nawaz Sharif and his government by every trick in the playbook of dirty politics, dharmas, marches, political diatribes, and relentless accusations, the super ambitious Imran Khan, the chief of PTI Party (Pakistan Tehreek e Instill) and his political sidekick, Sheikh Rasheed, filed a petition before the Pakistan Supreme Court in August 2016, seeking to disqualify Prime Minister Nawaz Sharif from holding public office since he was guilty of money laundering and corruption as was revealed by public disclosures of the Panama Papers and was thus dishonest (*sadiq* and *ameen*) under Article 62(1)(f) of the constitution. [18]

The roots of the Panama case against Nawaz Sharif go back to the incorporation of offshore companies by many prominent personalities across the world in the tax haven of Panama island. In April of 2016, the International Consortium of Investigative Journalists got hold of the confidential list of many world leaders compiled by the Panama law firm Mossback Finesse, including Pakistani prime minister Nawaz Sharif, who were the real owners of many such offshore companies.

Initially, the Supreme Court under Chief Justice Nisar in a short order had correctly dismissed this petition as being "prima facie frivolous" since it wasn't substantiated by any facts and evidence. However, under pressure Nisar relented and admitted the petition, even though it was inadmissible for hearing before the Supreme Court because of a lack of standing, jurisdiction, and other grounds. (See the analysis that follows.) In April 2017, the Supreme Court in a split decision ordered the formation of a joint investigation team (JIT) to institute inquiries into the allegations of Nawaz Sharif's corruption and money laundering.

After the submission of the JIT's report, on July 8, 2017, the Supreme Court under Chief Justice Nisar rendered the final verdict on this Panama Papers case, disqualifying the prime minister from membership in the national assembly and from holding any public office for life as he was deemed dishonest or more precisely was not *sadiq* or *ameen* pursuant to Article 62(1)(f) of the constitution because of his failing to disclosure to the election commission his Dubai-based employment contract with Capital FZE Company. The court also recommended that the NAB (National Bureau of Accountability) proceed with three references of corruption against Nawaz Sharif. As a follow-up to this judgment, the court also subsequently barred him from holding any public office for life under Article 62(1)(f).

Interestingly, in October 2018, the same Chief Justice Nisar dismissed a similar petition filed by politician Hanif Abbasi against Prime Minister Imran Khan, seeking Khan's disqualification since "no lawful point has been raised in the petition" regarding Khan's alleged nondisclosure of foreign funds of his PTI Party and of assets and ownership of an offshore company.

Avenfield Videogate

Even though the Supreme Court headed by Saqib Nasir in the previously outlined Panama Papers judgment of July 8, 2017, could not find Nawaz Sharif guilty of corruption charges, it thought fit to direct the NAB to file charges against the ex-prime minister and to constitute a joint investigation team (JIT) to investigate this corruption. This was strange because in common law jurisdictions such as Pakistan, judges are supposed to act as neutral arbiters to decide cases on the basis of evidence submitted before it and not assume the role of a zealous prosecutors. [22]

Avenfield Properties refer to four high-priced apartments worth about seven million pounds and located in London's prime Hyde Park neighborhood. The real estate was revealed by the notorious Panama Papers leaks in 2017, and they were allegedly owned by some shell companies formed by the Sharif family. After the NAB's filing of four corruption charges against the Sharif family on September 8, 2017, and submission of in investigative report by the JIT, the NAB court conducted his trial on these charges. On July 3, 2018, the NAB court rendered its verdict, and Sharif was found not guilty of corruption in view of a lack of evidence and money trail regarding acquisition and ownership of Avenfield Properties. However, this accountability court convicted Sharif on Kafkaesque, ambiguous grounds of "living beyond his means" and was sentenced to ten years in prison, a sentence that he is currently undergoing.

According to a confessional video released on July 13, 2019, Arshad

Malik, the NAB judge who rendered the said Avenfield verdict, was allegedly coerced and blackmailed by the authorities into finding Sharif guilty of living beyond means and sentencing him to ten years in jail. If indeed this turns out to be true, then the most honorable thing for the apex court, which ordered the referral to the NAB, or the Islamabad High Court would be to set aside the NAB verdict and Sharif's conviction. A retrial would not be feasible in view of the constitution bar on double jeopardy.

Election Act Decision

Following the Supreme Court verdict against Prime Minister Nawaz Sharif that disqualified him from membership in the national assembly and from holding the office of prime minister, the country's national assembly passed the amended Election Act (2017) so as to forestall his being also disqualified by Nisar's court as chief of his political party, the PMLN. However, this wasn't the case. The Supreme Court admitting political petitions against the amended Election Act also disqualified Nawaz Sharif from being the chief of his party in a judgment in February 2018. Saqib Nisar's decision in the infamous Election Act case against Prime Minister Nawaz Sharif that barred him from being the head of his political party was nothing but a brazen violation of the Pakistan Constitution, stretching the constitutional ambit to limits beyond its pale.

The Supreme Court asserted, "(U)under Article 63-A of the Constitution, the position of a Party Head of a political party that has a representation in, inter alia in the Parliament has a central role in the performance of duties by the Members of the Parliament." The court goes one step further and holds that "the Party Head must necessarily possess the qualifications and be free of the disqualifications of Article 62 and 63 of the Constitution."

First, such a holding was inconsistent with the well-established principle of supremacy of a written constitution. In a written constitution such as ours, the judiciary is bound to respect and obey the constitution in its current form and is restricted to what is actually provided within the four corners of its text. And what is not provided in the text, such as qualifications pertaining to a party head, cannot be written into it by judicial fiat on any pretext.

In that case, not only in Articles 62, 63, and 63-A but in the entire constitution, there was no mention of the qualifications, disqualifications, duties, or appointment of a party head of a political party other than a brief mention of a party head's duty under Article 63-A(1) to file a declaration of defection of a member of parliament with the election commission and to issue a show cause notice to that member. In its mission to interpret the constitution to determine the fate of a disqualified party head, the apex court was barking up the wrong tree.

Second, the ruling seemed to violate the fundamental principle of separation of powers of the three branches of the government pursuant to which only the legislative branch is empowered to amend or add any other provision or matter in the constitution. The judiciary's role is merely to interpret the constitution and not to advocate and institute changes in it, however well-intentioned or persuasive they might be.

The provisions of Articles 62 and 63 were specifically meant only for members of parliament and not for party heads. The new addition and application of Articles 62 and 63 for the qualifications and disqualifications of party heads amounts to an amendment to our constitution, which we all know can only be affected by our legislative branch and not by the judicial branch in accordance with the previously outlined principle of separation powers.

Third, in conformity with the established cannons of constitutional construction, the subject of the title or caption of an article or sub article is crucial in interpreting its substantive text. The title of Article 62 is "Qualifications for membership of Majlis-e-Shore (Parliament)." The title of Article 63 is "Disqualifications for membership of Parliament." And the title of Article 63-A is "Disqualifications (for memberships of Parliament) on grounds of defection."

It was clear that all these articles pertained specifically and exclusively to the topic of qualifications and disqualifications for membership of the parliament. They cannot be twisted and transposed to include the qualifications and disqualifications for party heads of a political party, which is exactly what our Supreme Court via this ruling is mandating us to do.

Fourth, in its hell-bent mission to insert the qualifications or disqualifications for a party head in the constitution, especially when it was not included by the framers of the constitution, the learned court was clearly barking up the wrong tree. It improperly invoked morality, religion, the Muslim faith, the "Islamic ideology," the "objectives resolution," the doomsday party head as a "kingmaker," and even "the integrity of Pakistan" in this endeavor. These misplaced arguments might have been valid and persuasive but only in the context of deliberations in the parliament if the legislators were debating to enact an amendment in our constitution to provide for qualifications and disqualification for a party head.

These arguments, however passionate or overpowering, could not be used by the court for what effectively amounts to amending the constitution. Whether right or wrong, in our Pakistan Constitution, the subject matter of qualifications or disqualifications for the head of a political party is left out. But it cannot be made a part of the constitution via judicial interpretation on any ground such as the Islamic ideology or morality.

Fifth, a harmonious or a holistic reading of the constitution that weaves together its disparate provisions (as noted previously) cannot add substantive provisions lacking intent of its framers. As far as the Election Act of 2017 with its amendment is concerned, neither the presence nor absence of a non obstante clause could affect the operation of this act by the parliament, the supreme lawmaking body.

Sixth, it's a basic principle of constitutional law that adjudication of political issues is deemed outside the realm of judicial interpretation. Can anyone doubt that the matter of qualification and appointment of the head of a political party is inherently not political in nature? Matters of politics and political parties are generally inadmissible for hearing in a court of law, *suo moto* Article 184(3) jurisdiction or not. Indeed, there are practical considerations as to why political party issues such as qualifications and appointments of officers of political parties are inadmissible and nonjusticiable for a hearing in the courts of law.

For instance, these deliberations would inevitably open up a hornet's nest, a floodgate of political litigation to swamp our judicial system, besides imposing an almost unbearable task on our already overburdened courts to lay out and sustain judicially managed standards and rules for the functioning of political parties. One may agree with the court's belief that heads of political parties conducting parliamentary business must be "persons of probity, integrity and high moral character." But that determination is made by the people through laws enacted by their chosen representatives in the parliament rather than by the judiciary.

Seventh—and regretfully—this judgment was also wrong on another constitutional ground. It impinged upon the basic freedom of association and the fundamental right of citizens to form and establish political parties with terms of their choice under Article 17 of our constitution.

Finally, if Pakistan laws and our constitution are somehow thought to be deficient in any respect, then we must remember the adage that we have to live and abide by the constitution we have and not by the constitution we wish we had—that is, until we change it.

Mughal King

By the end of his tumultuous term, Nisar lost any sense of judicial restraint, stalking the land and dispensing *suo moto* justice like a Mughal king. He made impromptu visits to hospitals, schools, restaurants, courts, offices to issue on-the-spot orders. He declared himself to be on a mission to deliver "clean air, clean water and pure milk" to the citizens. With no legal basis, he started raising and cajoling money for the construction of a huge ($14 billion) water dam, and when he was able to raise barely a tiny fraction of the cost of this dam, he said that he only wanted to raise an awareness of the water problem in the country. In any other country, that would have been a clear case of racketeering and fraud. Interfering in commercial and privatization decisions of the executive government and voiding international arbitration contracts of foreign investors with Pakistan and local government, he along with

Chief Justice Iftikhar directly or indirectly caused losses of billions of dollars to the nation.

Outrageous PKLI and Turkish Cases

It would be remiss not to point out to a few stunning illustrations of Saqib Nisar's cavalier approach to and utter disregard of his supreme judicial duties. Once he walked in an ongoing session of a district court in Sindh not unlike the bullying sheriff of the old Wild West barging through the swinging doors of a salon, ridiculing the terrified judge who was conducting the hearing and throwing out his cell phone. In March 2018, he single-handedly dismantled a much-needed state-of-the-art health care institute, Lahore's Pakistan Kidney and Liver Institute (PKLI), which was pioneering the transplants of livers and kidneys in Pakistan, was established though the dedication and sacrifices of a few altruistic and highly qualified Pakistan American physicians who wanted to give something back to the land of their origin. On the prodding of his envious brother, who worked as a physician in a public hospitable, Nisar as chief justice took *suo moto* notice of the internal functions of PKLI entity on the ground that the salaries of its private physicians were higher than those of government physicians, and in an order, he disbanded the legal governing board of PKLI, nominated his own committee to replace the board, put PKLI's chief, the notable Dr. Akhtar Saeed, on the exit control list, and ordered a forensic audit.

Another case that defied logic or justice involved Turkey and its president, Erdogan. Pakistan Turkey Educational Foundation (PTEF), a Turkish educational foundation inspired by Turkish leader Fethullah Gulen, Erdogan's political rival, established a chain of schools in Pakistan to impart needed, quality education. Seeking a political vendetta against his rival, President Erdogan had made it clear to Pakistan government his displeasure over the existence of these schools. To make a long story short, Nisar, in a bid to placate Erdogan, took *suo moto* notice of PTEF on December 13, 2018, although this case was already pending. Disregarding their rights to due process of the lawfully established PTEF, he declared it a terrorist organization and ordered the freezing of its bank accounts and confiscation of its assets. He then transferred its functioning to another entity without any proof or a trial. No wonder two days later Nisar was in Turkey being feted by Erdogan himself, who must have been jumping with joy in his ability to make the chief justice of a foreign country dance to his tune. A grim reminder that an unchecked and unbridled judiciary can easily turn into a legalized tyranny.

Trampling Constitutional Free Speech

Article 19 of the Pakistan Constitution says, "Every citizen shall have the right to freedom of speech and expression, and there shall be freedom of the press, subject to any restrictions imposed by law."

It's well documented that Pakistan has become one of the world's most dangerous place for journalists and reporters. In a July 2018 interview with the *Washington Post*, Hameed Haroon, owner of Pakistan's most prestigious newspaper, *DAWN*, opined that "an unprecedented assault by the Pakistan Military on the freedom of the press" was underway. This assault on the press was an assault on the constitution, specifically on the previously outlined Article 19. [19]

Credit for this ignominy mostly goes to the ubiquitous military or its hirelings with the judiciary generally as silent spectators. According to a UNESCO country report, at least fifty-seven journalists in Pakistan have been killed since 2010 in their professional line of duty. Among the most notables journalists and reporters targeted were: Geo TV popular anchor Hamid Mir in 2014 (attacked by proxy assassins on motor bikes), Salim Shahzad in 2011 (his tortured body dumped in a canal), Gohar Wazir in 2019 (attacked by killers in KPK), *Dawn's* top journalist, Cyril Almeida in 2018 [21] (the government filing treason charges for his reporting of a civil government and military meeting). Incidentally, Almeida was awarded the prestigious 2019 World Press Freedom Hero Award by the International Press Institute). In its September 2018 report, the Committee for the Protection of Journalists (CPJ) stated, "As does killings of journalists in Pakistan decline so too does freedom, as the country's powerful military quietly but effectively, restricts reporting by barring access, encouraging self-censorship though direct and indirect intimidation, and even allegedly instigating violence against reporters." [20]

In a relentless drive by the Pakistan government to stifle dissent and criticism of its policies and political oppression, many of the reputed TV anchors and writers were purged, and the media houses were subjected to relentless economic pressure and intimidation. Though the judiciary had no direct hand in muzzling of free speech and free media, in trampling the constitutional guarantees of freedom of expression, the Pakistani rulers proceeded on the tacit assumption (which turned out to be the case) that the Supreme Court would acquiesce in these violations of human rights, turning a blind eye.

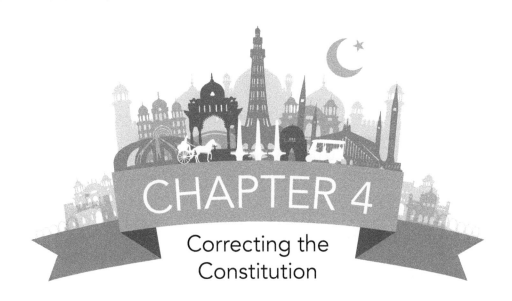

CHAPTER 4

Correcting the Constitution

Eliminate Constitutional Hodgepodge

With their frequent injections of whimsical, inconsistent, and self-serving provisions by despots, dictators, and greedy politicians, Pakistani constitutions have been reduced to political schizophrenic document. In this respect, the 1956 constitution passed by the constituent assembly appeared to be most democratic. The 1962 constitution with its centerpiece of basic democracy was no more than a dictator's wish list to perpetuate his rule. The 1973 constitution was genuinely promulgated, though it contained certain unsustainable provisions out of political expediency [1]. But sadly, its restored version was mutilated by General Zia's tyrannical Article 58(2)(b) and religious diktats, though subsequent regimes have tried to mitigate some of the damage done to it by enacting amendments, most notable the Seventeenth and Eighteenth Amendments. Notwithstanding, the 1973 constitution is still a hodgepodge of anomalies, contradictions, and ambiguities, a badly drafted contextual text if ever there was one. [2]

Perhaps an ideal constitution for ethnically diverse Pakistan would have been the stellar, secular constitution of South Africa. Though these frenzied, extremely religious despondent eras are not conducive for a rational, modern dispensation, such a move might have avoided the religious bloodbath, political upheavals, and economic distress this nation has been subjected to for decades. In order to sweep the existing Islamized constitution and replace it with a completely secular order may be unpragmatic as the nation has drifted too far in the direction of fundamentalism, given the dangerously low level of education in the country and the precarious political and economic stability at present. Religious passions and frenzy run deep, and they have seeped into the bone morrow of many of Pakistan's citizens. It would be very difficult to completely dislodge this entrenched indoctrination at this point. In the words of Humera Iqtidar and David Gilmartin, two researchers of the Pakistani state and secularism, "Pakistan occupies an uncertain problematic space in debates over secularism."

No doubt that the current 1973 constitution in its mutilated version by Gen Zia is full of loopholes, inconsistencies, contradictions with a spurious mixture of religion and secular that it requires a major surgery.[3] Having said that, a complete repudiation of the entire document is neither feasible nor suggested. for the reasons stated previously [4]

A constitution is a beacon light to point the nation toward the country's future direction and a navigational tool to steer it toward the shores of its national vision. Its provisions should be dynamic, unifying, and forward-looking to keep abreast with other nations in this modern era but also for the prosperity, progress, and general welfare of its people. On the contrary, a deficient constitution that has glaring defects such as discriminatory clauses against a section of the citizens or regressive provisions loses respect and credibility with the people. Its very legitimacy as a sublime, sacrosanct, prime inspiration and a unifying and motivational force that can take the country forward is threatened. Consequently, the sooner its shortcomings—as pointed out previously and elsewhere in this book—are resolved and dealt with the sooner its full legitimacy and credibility would be restored.

Be that as it may, a constitution is the core document of a country. It's the engine of growth and progress of a nation-state. It sets its direction and pace. [5] The present constitution, namely the 1973 constitution, is not sustainable in its present shape and form. It's a roadblock to the country's growth and progress. Consequently, the following constitutional steps that involve modification of the constitution's most egregious and incompatible provisions and elimination of loopholes are essential for the country to move forward on the right course.[6]

Streamline Constitutional Text

A democratic constitution draws its legitimacy from the will of the people based on its consensus. The finality, resoluteness, and the high moral ground inherent in a constitution elicit not only reverence but also its obedience and deference by citizens. Unfortunately, the Pakistan Constitution is not among the best constitutions of the democratic world. It has quite a few loopholes and much imprecise, inconsistent language in its text that results in some unintended consequences and political uncertainty in the country. A quick review of the Pakistan Constitution seems to indicate that most of its provisions that bestow rights and distribute power are conditional, qualified, and transient rather than final and unequivocal.[7] It's a tortured, recalcitrant document that requires prompt rectification of such blemishes as indicated here.[8]

Some provisions in the constitution contain the restrictive phrases such as "subject to law," "subject to the Constitution," or "in accordance with law." To illustrate this, see Article 22(3), which pertains to "Safeguards as to education institutions in respect to religion, etc." It states that "*Subject to law* (emphasis added) ... no religious community or denomination shall be prohibited from providing religious instruction for pupil of that community or denomination." But which law? An existing law or some future law? Second, why would a constitutional provision be subjected to any law? Isn't it the other way around? Shouldn't the law be subject to and in compliance with the constitution? In legal hierarchy, a constitutional provision is higher than an ordinary law. The constitution is the supreme, controlling law of the land of Pakistan, which cannot be made subservient to any law on the statute books. A law is declared illegal if it violates any of the constitutional provisions. This clause is not the only one in the Pakistan Constitution that includes the qualification of being "subject to law." There are other similar clauses that needs to be modified.

Similarly, Article 17(3), which concerns the freedom of association, states, "Every political party shall account for the source of its funds *in accordance with law* (emphasis added)." The italicized phrase seems redundant. Indeed, if there's an existing law that requires political parties to report their accounting, it's their legal duty to comply with the law, constitutional provision or not. Moreover, Article 90(1) on the federal government states, *"Subject to the Constitution* (emphasis added), the executive authority of the Federation shall be exercised in the name of the President by the Federal Government." Here, a provision of the constitution, which is a part of the constitution itself, avers that its contents are "subject to the constitution." Really? Isn't every provision in the constitution subject to it? This is an acute perception of the very obvious indeed!

The most sweeping and self-defeating constitutional provision is perhaps the Article 227(1) clause, which admonishes, "(A)ll existing laws shall be brought in conformity with the Injunctions of Islam as laid down in the Quran and Sunnah." In one stroke this improper and ill-advised clause seems to dampen the permanence of country's laws and preeminence of the constitution. In other words, according to this provision, all Pakistani laws should be seen as temporary, ad hoc, or uncertain in nature until their bona fides are confirmed to be in line with Islamic injunctions. A constitutional dilemma would arise if a law were to be passed that confirmed to Islamic Injunctions but violated the provisions of the Constitution. Moreover, what exactly are the injunctions of Islam? The list of all Islamic injunctions is too broad, too wide-ranging with varied interpretations as to be amenable to a uniform, universal, indisputable, and final application.

There are at least two clauses that notoriously stand out—Article 62(1)(f) and Article 184(3). Article 62(1)(f) provides that a person is not qualified for being a national assembly member unless "he is sagacious, righteous and non-profligate, honest and ameen." The words used in this clause, namely righteous, honest, and *ameen*, are too broad and incapable of a precise meaning. As a basic principle of constitutional construction, any ambiguous and overly broad language is deemed improper and disregarded. So too, the use of the word *he* without adding *she* is improper since there are women who serve as national assembly members. These laconic words have far-reaching legal and political consequences. For example, recently in the Panama case against the former prime minister Nawaz Sharif, the Supreme Court banned him from politics for life because he was not honest or ameen. Hence, this provision along with Article 62(1)(d) should be stricken or revised and substituted.

Along similar lines, Article 184(3) should be discarded or substantially modified since jurisdiction given to the Supreme Court to entertain cases on its own motion if there arises "a question of public importance with respect to the enforcement of enforcement of the Fundamental Rights" is too broad, giving the apex court almost limitless powers to hear any case.

Some constitutional purists might argue against the inclusion of clear and express provisions relating to separation of powers, inadmissibility of political questions in the courts, legitimization of military coups and overthrows of democratic governments, outlawing doctrine of necessity, among other assertions in the Pakistan Constitution on the grounds that modern, democratic constitutions do not contain such specificity. This assertion might be true to some extent, but democratic counties in this age have firmly established democratic norms and traditions that respect the constitution and rule of law and have highly educated, politically sophisticated, rational societies—imperatives that are sorely lacking in a half-literate, frenzied, feudal Pakistan with predatory institutions.

Discard Constitutional Discrimination

Expressly and unabashedly banning non-Muslim citizens from ever assuming the highest political offices in the land, namely as the president and prime minister, is perhaps the most offensive provision in the Pakistan Constitution. On the one hand, it guarantees equality to all citizens, but on the other hand, it brazenly takes it away too. Article

25(1) provides that "all citizens are equal before law and are entitled to equal protection of law." But Article 41(2) states, "(A) person shall not be qualified for election as President unless he is a Muslim." In a similar vein, Article 91(3) says, "After the election of the Speaker and the Deputy Speaker. the National Assembly shall ... proceed to elect without debate one of its *Muslim* (emphasis added) members to be the Prime Minister." This open discrimination against minority citizens not only violates the equal protection guaranteed in the constitution itself but also flouts international law and the UN Declaration of Human Rights, which outlaw's discrimination based on religious belief. These discriminatory clauses have to go. There is no other option. Otherwise, they will always block any attempt by the nation to march forward.

Civilian-Military Clarity

It's no secret that civil-military relationship in Pakistan has been contentious and confusing at times rather than smooth and optimum. Apart from the political tussle for power and dominance over policy matters between the civilian government and the military hierarchy, a lack of constitutional clarity over the command and reporting structure has also significantly contributed to the friction between the two entities. Regarding command of the Pakistan's Armed Forces, Article 243(1) of the Constitution stipulates, "The Federal Government shall have control and command of the Armed Forces." Article 243(2) provides, "Without prejudice to the generality of the foregoing, the Supreme Command of the Armed Forces shall vest in the President." These provisions destroy the unity of control and command of the national forces, which is so crucial in war and peace, first by having two types of commands, specifically general command and supreme command. Second, because multiple entities have control and command, the president and the federal government actually consists of the prime minister and the federal ministers (Article 90(1)).

Civilian and military relations are further fractured by the indirect reporting process by the chiefs of the army, the navy, and the air force. Instead of requiring them to report directly to the prime minister, who is the chief executive of the federal government, the chiefs have to report first to the secretary of the Ministry of Defense, who in turn reports to the minister of defense, who in turn reports to the prime minister. This must change in the Constitution. To promote unity of command and control of the armed forces and to foster supremacy of the civilian government over the military, the office of the prime minister must be clearly and unequivocally thus empowered. To remove all doubt as to who is in charge of the armed forces in a country prone to army chiefs seizing political power, it might not be imprudent for the Constitution to state that the prime minister shall be the supreme commander of all the armed forces of the country.

Moreover, neither Article 243 or any other provision of the Constitution the Army Act or its Regulations law expressly provides for the extension of the terms of Chiefs of the Army, Navy and Air Force or Chairman, Joint Chiefs of Staff Committee. This provision pertains to the appointment of these Chiefs while the subject of their extensions by the Government is not provided anywhere in the Constitution. It was indeed shocking that many Army Chiefs in the history of the country have been given extra constitutionally extensions of service when their tenures had duly expired. If the Government wants power to grant the Chiefs extensions of service then the Constitution (or specifically Article 243) must be amended accordingly in order to give the Parliament the required constitutional umbrella to pass a new legislation for granting extension or for amending the existing Army Act.

In a republic like Pakistan, its written constitution is the supreme law of the land: any legislative act of the Parliaments must confirm to the written text of the Constitution. If it doesn't then it would be in violation of the Constitution and would be declared null and void. That's why in countries which have a written constitution many laws are challenged in the courts on the grounds of their being ultra vires or failing to adhere to the constitutional provisions. Yes, the Parliament can pass any law as long as it confirms to the provisions of the Constitution. In the extension case, the law under consideration, revision of Army Act, or a new legislation allowing extensions for Services Chiefs, would exceed the limit of appointment set by the

Constitution, then the Parliament must first duly amend the pertinent provision of the Constitution, which in this case would be Article 243, Without a constitutional cover no act of parliament can pass the legal muster. Finally, if the Army Act is amended or a new legislative act is passed by the Parliament without first changing the Constitution, it would be overturned by the Supreme Court on the grounds of it being inconsistent with the Constitution on a petition to the Court.

Revisit Objectives Resolution

Sometimes the thoughtless actions of politicians in a nascent democracy have a profound effect on a country's policy, well-being, and future. The Objectives Resolution adopted by Pakistan's constituent assembly in March 1949 during the premiership of Liaquat Ali Khan was such a thoughtless and irresponsible political act.[2] The mere language of this document turns any legal drafting on its head. It's so full of inconsistencies, contradictions, redundancies, and ambiguities. It was drafted by a history professor named Ishtiaq Hussain Qureshi, who had no legal education or training. However, it was General Zia who in 1985 incredibly institutionalized this spurious document and gave it a legal force by making it a part and parcel of the main provisions of the Constitution as Article 2A. And ever since no attempts have been made to discard it though many governments have come and gone.

To give an example of the rhetorical nature and constitutional imprudence of the Objectives Resolution, let's look at clauses 5 and 9. Clause 5 states, "The principles of democracy, freedom, equality, tolerance and social justice, as enunciated by Islam, shall be fully observed." Clause 9 then states, "Fundamental rights shall be guaranteed. They include equality of status, of opportunity and (sic) before law, social, economic and political justice, and freedom of thought, expression, belief, faith, worship and association subject to law and public morality." This appears redundant and inconsistent. What if the fundamental rights that are constitutionally *guaranteed* conflict with the principle of democracy, which is the case with the Islamic concept of equality before law? Then which takes precedence? The democratic principle or Islamic injunctions? Consequently, the place of the objectives resolution in its present form should be reconsidered.

In view of the previously outlined inconsistencies and theocratic as well as emotional intrusion into the constitution, the Objectives Resolution may be deleted, or upon the insistence of zealous purveyors of Islamist ideology to keep it in the main text of the constitution, its language may be revised accordingly.

Redefine Separation of Powers

In practical terms the basic purpose of the constitution is to provide a system and scope for good governance. In Pakistan, we have to lay down the basic ground rules and structure for governance while protecting the rights of the citizens. One of the fundamental rules enshrined in the Pakistan Constitution is the principle of the separation of the three branches of the government—the executive, the judiciary, and the legislature. Each branch is limited by a system of checks and balances. The underlying purpose of such separation of powers is to prevent the imposition of a tyrannical rule on the people. Unfortunately, as Pakistan history bears witness, this has not always been the case. One of the main causes has been the constitution itself. The separation of powers has not been clearly defined and demarcated, and the checks and balances lack clarity and sharpness. These inherent inadequacies within the constitution must be addressed and spelled out to remove any doubts.

Revise Freedom of Speech Text

As enunciated previously, Article 19 should be revised since it has obviously failed to provide meaningful freedom of speech and freedom of the press as it has been subjected to many abuses. Another clause may be added that enumerates various types of prohibited direct and indirect abuses as well as manipulations and violations of the freedom of expression by the government, including the military.

Tackle Judicial Activism

Much has been said and much has been written on the menace of judicial activism of Pakistan's Supreme Court, but hardly any worthwhile, effective solutions other than platitudes of restraint have been offered to curb the menace. When we speak of judicial activism, we tend to speak in broad spectrums, although in actuality, its Pakistani version is more egregious and audacious than what is generally implied in democratic countries.

For instance, in the United States, judicial activism involves expansion of fundamental rights guaranteed by the US Constitution. It was epitomized by the decision in the *Roe v. Wade* case where the US Supreme Court expanded the constitutional right of privacy to include the penumbra right to have an abortion, even though the right was not provided in that way in the US Constitution. But judicial activism of Pakistan Supreme Court is more like judicial adventurism as it erodes some of the bedrock principles on which our constitution and republic are based.

Judicial activism that is practiced in Pakistan by its Supreme Court may be classified into two broad categories. The first category concerns the Supreme Court's interpretation and misuse of *suo moto* provision of Article184(3) of the constitution as a limitless jurisdiction and power to issue orders on any matter under the sun on the pretext of enforcement of fundamental rights—Chief Justice Iftikhar and Chief Justice Saqib Nisar being its celebrity practitioners.

The second category of the Supreme Court's judicial activism, political interference, has seen a long history of meddling in the political domain, dismissing heads of governments, and legitimizing,

A two- pronged constitutional solution is proposed below for the elimination or reduction of the said judicial dilemma. Many observers have dubbed it as the judicialization of Pakistani politics, a dangerous trend that would undermine the rule of law.

1. Sue Moto Solution

Jurisdiction is the authority given to various courts by law or constitution to hear and decide a case. Basically, there are two kinds of jurisdiction—appellate jurisdiction and original jurisdiction. Appellate jurisdiction is the authority of courts to review and decide cases or disputes on appeal from lower courts or tribunals- Article 185 of Pakistan Constitution. Original jurisdiction is the power of courts to hear and decide a case or dispute that comes directly before it for resolution for the first time.

In Pakistan, the original jurisdiction conferred on our supreme court is restricted to disputes or cases between the federal and provincial government(s) (see Article 184(1) of Pak Constitution). In our Pakistani Constitution, original jurisdiction has been expanded to include the so-called *suo moto* jurisdiction as per Article 184(3)—the subject matter of the present discussion. Such jurisdiction gives the Supreme Court the power to initiate cases for hearing and adjudication on its own motion or on its own cognizance-*suo moto*- without the cases first started by a prosecutor in a trial court as is the norm in a legal system.

The controversial provision of Article 184(3) of the Constitution, often called the *suo moto* jurisdiction, empowers the Pakistan Supreme Court to assume original jurisdiction and hear and decide cases "if it considers a question of public importance with respect to the enforcement of the Fundamental Rights (as specific in Ch 1, Part 11 of the Constitution) is involved," and accordingly, they can make an appropriate order. The democratic constitution is based on the pillar of the separation of the three branches of the government, namely the executive, legislature, and judiciary. Its further underpinned on the inalienable rights and freedoms guaranteed therein, such as that of due process, including the right of a fair trial, the right of appeal, the right to a jury, the right of a neutral arbiter, etc.

Besides tarnishing the image of the country, such exercise of excessive and unfettered power of the judiciary destroys the costly, nationwide election process as well as the mandate, aspirations, and choices of millions of citizens for self-governance. It is these bedrock principles of our republic that are threatened by this ill-advised *suo moto* jurisdiction given to our Supreme Court. Let's examine why.

First, the overly broad language of this *suo moto* provision as a "question of public importance with respect to the enforcement of the Fundamental Rights" is inconsistent with the basic rules of drafting constitutional text. Under this doctrine clauses that are too broad or ambiguous have been deemed unconstitutional since they are not conducive to precise interpretation and a single meaning.

Second, the sweeping nature of the scope of *suo moto* jurisdiction gives unfettered, almost limitless jurisdiction to our apex court since any matter under the sun can be interpreted as a "question of public importance with respect to the enforcement of Fundamental Rights." Indeed, the Supreme Court has interpreted this text so that the members can hear and rule on matters including the price of samosas, the management of a hospital, the appointment of corporate officers, the performance of sports teams, and the dismissal of parliamentarians and chief executives of the country.

Third and more importantly, the wide jurisdiction has led the Supreme Court toward diluting and usurping the separate, exclusive powers of the other two branches of our democratic system, the executive and legislature, as enshrined in the constitution. Impulsive exercise of suo moto jurisdiction weakens and undermines rather than strengthens various institutions of our country, including the judiciary itself. The leapfrogging over lower courts in pursuit of 'sue mottos' sends a loud message to the people that our lower courts are incapable of delivering justice, thus weakening the institution of the judiciary.

On the other hand, our endeavor should be to ensure that the entire country's court system is confident, strong, and capable enough and accessible to protect and enforce fundamental rights of even the disenfranchised citizens. The judiciary's interference through *suo moto* hearings in the deliberations of the national assembly, ruling on qualification or disqualification of the members and on internal matters of parliamentary affairs, encroaches upon the exclusive legislative power of the parliament. Such actions have resulted in casting doubt and disrespecting the legislative enactments, undermining the plenary powers of the legislative branch to make laws and supremacy of the legislative branch.

It wouldn't be hyperbolic to assert that the apex court exercising its *suo moto* jurisdiction at times seems to dampen the constitutional powers of the executive branch to implement the laws and run the country effectively. In suo moto notices, the Supreme Court has interfered in and negated proper functions of the executive government such as appointment of officials, administration of bureaucracy, and government entities. Chief Justice Saqib Nisar acted like a de facto government or a super prime minister, second-guessing, overriding the proper actions of the executive government, and even removing prime ministers and dismissing government officials.

Fourth, we should never underestimate the cloud of political instability and the resultant economic uncertainty and downturn that the one-size-fits-all suo moto sledgehammer creates. Serial dismissals of elected prime ministers and parliamentarians by judicial fiat and suo moto trickery is not a simple matter without disastrous consequences for the country.

Besides tarnishing the image of the country, such exercise of excessive and unfettered power of the judiciary destroys the nationwide election process as well as the mandate, aspirations, and choice of millions of citizens for self-governance. It erodes the sovereignty of the people to rule themselves while conflating the judiciary as a kind of super government lording over the duly elected government of the people. It is time to save the judiciary from itself. We must either completely abolish the anomalous, overarching suo moto jurisdiction or modify its scope. Judges are not chief executives, social reformers, or policemen.

Fifth, in the realm of politics and political affairs, the invocation of the *suo moto* jurisdiction by the apex court is most egregious. The saga of Panama-related cases that stemmed from the trilogy of sue moto actions against the elected prime minister has painfully highlighted this issue. It's a basic principle of adjudication that questions of political nature or political parties are nonjusticiable and courts are barred from hearing them. Yet our apex court disqualified and removed Nawaz

Sharif as head of the PLMN Party, which was a purely political issue. In the third Panama case, the Supreme Court of Saqib Nisar barred prime minister Nawaz Sharif for life from contesting any political election despite the nonexistence of a prior declaration by the court about his lack of honesty, which declaration was a prerequisite under Article 62(1)(f) of the Constitution.

Sixth, the judiciary's recourse to suo moto jurisdiction has resulted in infringements on individuals' due process rights and ironically, the very fundamental rights the Supreme Court purports to protect. Our constitution guarantees certain due process rights to citizens, such as the right to a fair trial, judgment by a neutral and unbiased arbiter, the assumption of innocence until proven guilty, the right of appeal, etc. All such rights are trampled upon by a suo moto action where the judge is also the prosecutor and jury as well.

Seventh, it would be remiss not to point out that the original jurisdiction bestowed to apex courts by law in democratic nations is quite limited and is sparingly exercised. In fact, no constitution of any democratic country contains such a suo moto provision in the shape and form that exists in Article 184(3). For instance, the US Constitution does not contain any such suo moto provision, though the US Supreme Court has the power to issue some prerogative writs, for the main purpose of enforcing its own orders. The original jurisdiction of the mighty Supreme Court is restricted to cases mainly involving foreign consuls and to those cases in which a state is a party (Article 111, clause 2).

Having good intentions or not, judges should not be allowed to substitute via legal mechanism their own policies, social ideas or political philosophy for the right of people to govern themselves. A reign of a structured legal system should not be supplanted by an erratic, uncertain reign of *suo motos*.

In India, the Supreme Court (and also the high courts) have suo moto original jurisdiction regarding an individual's fundamental rights under Articles 32 and 226 of the Indian Constitution, but it's restricted to cases in which the court lacks subject-matter jurisdiction. Furthermore, unlike Pakistan's Article 184(3) jurisdiction, in India, only aggrieved persons can petition the apex court for *suo moto* action. Questions of public importance are not covered, and neither are matters pertaining to other constitutional provisions or other laws. Moreover, such power of the Indian Supreme Court is generally restricted to issuance of orders of specific writs pertaining to habeas corpus, mandamus, certiorari, and warrantor.

Eighth, there are pragmatic considerations such as having a limited number of judges on its bench and the sheer, burgeoning number of cases pending on its docket that makes it imperative for the Supreme Court to restrict hearing cases on its original jurisdiction.

If any party, whether actually injured or not, is allowed to file petitions and if the court on its own indulgence and initiative decides to entertain matters of ubiquitous infringements of fundamental rights in the country with endless "public importance" impact, it will open the floodgates of litigation in the Supreme Court.

It's not as if the Pakistan Supreme Court has cleared its docket of cases and is sitting idly and doodling. Actually. the court is swamped with thousands of pending cases (about forty thousand pending cases) languishing for decades to be heard. Abandoning its heavy workload, the apex court has recklessly jumped, flush with the suo moto adrenaline, on hundreds of populist matters, distracting its attention and resources from its regular burgeoning docket.

Not only does the sheer volume of unfinished cases need urgent attention, but the Supreme Court's unwise and thoughtless intervention via suo moto has resulted in huge monetary losses to the nation in such niche cases as *Reko Diq* arbitration (loss of about $10 billion), TTI Turkish Power Boats rental ($800 million loss), PSM privatization (loss of Rs 300 billion so far), PIA privatization (continuing loss), Asaf Pain illegal taxation (loss undetermined), etc.

Finally, some have argued that perhaps a modified version of Article 184(3) might work. It's possible—that is, if we can narrow down the scope of the nebulous suo moto jurisdiction to specific extraordinary remedies for special situations.

These remedies, drastically limiting the scope of the court's original Article 184(3) jurisdiction would provide relief not available elsewhere regarding the enforcement of certain fundamental rights such as the writ of habeas corpus (for enforced disappearances, unlawful arrests and detention, etc.), mandamus (for government officials to implement an order), writ of certiorari (to order submission of records for its judicial review of a case), and the power to enforce its own contempt of court orders.

We must either completely abolish the anomalous, overarching *suo moto* jurisdiction or modify its scope, but we must always keep in mind the adage that judges are not legislators. Having good intentions or not, judges should not be allowed to substitute via legal mechanism their own policies, social ideas, or political philosophy for the right of people to govern themselves. A reign of a structured legal system should not be supplanted by an erratic, uncertain reign of *suo motos*. It's a big fallacy to assume that the Supreme Court has the duty to enforce of fundamental rights of the citizens. It does not.

Judiciary enforces fundamental rights only in the course of hearing and resolving cases or disputes between adversaries that come before it. This is the duty and function of the executive branch rather than the judiciary to enforce and implement laws of the land, including fundamental rights. If Pakistan's democracy is to survive, if the people's power is to reign supreme, if our constitution is allowed to flourish and respected by all, we must begin with the fundamental principle that the function of our judiciary is to interpret the constitution and enforce laws only when it is asked to hear cases and resolve disputes. Nothing less, nothing more is required of the apex court. overthrows of our constitution.

2. Reducing Judicial Interference

One of the important reasons of the huge gridlock of pending cases in the judicial system is the propensity of the Supreme Court to hear cases that are intrinsically political in nature. Generally speaking, political issues are considered nonjusticiable in a court of law because meddling by the judiciary in political affairs causes political instability and infringement of the principle of separation of powers in the constitution. Indeed, Pakistan has experienced disastrous political upheaval in the wake of the Supreme Court's unwarranted adjudication of Panama cases involving the form prime minister Nawaz Sharif. The Pakistan Constitution must appropriately address this by outlawing political questions from the jurisdiction of the apex court, thus saving time, resources, political stability, judicial independence, neutrality, and restraint. Judiciary's interference in political matters took root as early as 1955, when in Saifuddin case, Chief Justice Munir justified the illegal dissolution of the assembly on the grounds of the doctrine of necessity. From then on, the doctrine assumed a life of its own in a stunning series of landmark cases. form, a constitutional amendment is needed that would either repeal or substantially modify this overly broad provision.

In order to eliminate or greatly reduce the judicial activism of the more pernicious, second category of judicial activism, perhaps passing another corresponding constitutional amendment should be enacted that would require some expert drafting and delicate balancing skills. Such an amendment would expressly bar the judiciary from removing or disqualifying an elected head of government (remedies to remove a prime minister are available in the parliament and among the electorate); interfering in executive functions; justifying or supporting subversion or the overthrow of the constitution or the government; adjudicating any matter involving political parties or political issues; and/or exceeding duty or power of the judiciary as laid down in the constitution. Some may argue that these provisions would be a bit harsh and overbearing on the judiciary. This might be true. But it's also true that our nation has suffered much in its long history of judicial excesses. Sometimes unique and drastic situations call for unique and drastic measures.

Remove *Shariat* Appellate Bench

While the establishment of an adjunct, specialized tribunal, such as the Federal *Shariat* Court pursuant to Article 203(F) of the constitution by the government and the parliament, is their rightful prerogative, creation of an appellate bench inside the Supreme Court is not. Article

203(F)(3) provides that to hear appeals from the Federal *Shariat* Court, "there shall be constituted *in* (emphasis added) the Supreme Court a Bench to be called the *Shariat* Appellate Bench," consisting of three Muslim judges of the Supreme Court plus two *Ulemas*. Such an appellate bench in the Supreme Court is neither permitted nor acceptable since it violates the exclusiveness, singularity, and sanctity of the apex court. A *Shariat* bench, appellate or not, cannot be made part of the Supreme Court bench. It's another matter that the Supreme Court appoint a bench to hear an appeal on a *Shariat* case.

CHAPTER 5
Pakistani Welfare Nationalism

Often things you think are just beginning are coming to an end.
--John Dos Passos

Why Nationalism?

Inculcation of pride, passion and performance for a state is what constitutes nationalism, the basis of the entity of a modern nation state. The defining trait of a nation-state is nationalism, and it is only appropriate that it is employed in holding the country together, uniting it as one nation and promoting its growth and cohesiveness. But what kind of a nationalism does the country need? That's the million-dollar question. [1]

Noted political theorist Yoram Hazony pinpoints the basic principles of a nation-state from which modern nationalism flows.[2] The state must be militarily strong to defend its independence and sovereignty. It must not interfere in the affairs of other states and respect their sovereignty. It must have a monopoly over coercive powers and weapons. It must offer protection for its minorities. It must protect the rights and freedom of individuals and must sanctify its written constitution. Nationalism legitimizes "the collective right of a free people to rule themselves."

Enunciated below is an analysis of the main variants of nationalism and the conclusion that Welfare Nationalism- Pakistani style- can be the motivational vehicle that can take this country forward to the next level of statehood, progress and development.

Muslim Nationalism

The roots of Muslim nationalism in the Indian subcontinent, from which sprang the idea of a separate state for Muslims,,[4] go as far back as late nineteenth century when the Muslim political activist and educationist in the British India Sir Syed Ahmed Khan highlighted the defeatist and backward plight of Muslims then and launched the Aligarh Movement in collaboration with a few Muslim feudal lords for the uplift of Muslims via education first, establishing the Aligarh University, the flag bearer of higher learning for Indian Muslims. In her thesis "Partitioning India: Indian Muslim Nationalism and the Origins of the Muslim State (1800–1947)," the research historian Sophie Buur then points to the next milestone in the evolution of Muslim nationalism: the All India Muslim League meeting held in Decca in 1906 when the demand for separate electorate for Indian Muslims was raised on the basis of their being a separate nation within a nation.[5] Though this meeting did not directly called for a separate Muslim state in India, but it sowed the seeds for Muslim nationalism there.

In the 1930s at Cambridge in the United Kingdom, when Britain was holding the first roundtable conferences of Hindu and Muslim political leaders, Ch Ramat Ali espoused that the growing Hindu-Muslim communal problem in India was not simply communal in nature but was really a matter of different nationalities of Hindus and Muslims, and he later floated the idea of a separate homeland for Muslims to be called Pakistan, an acronym for northwest provinces of the Indian subcontinent. [6]

In 1940, the twenty-first session of the Muslim League passed the Lahore Resolution, adopting the idea of Pakistan. It demanded that the Muslim majority region of northwest India be grouped together to form independent states that were autonomous and sovereign. According to Pakistan history expert Sharif ul Mujahid, three Muslim leaders of India, specifically Sir Syed Ahmed, Mohammad Ali Jinnah, and Mohammad Iqbal, were "responsible for carving out for the Muslims a separate identity and an independent state of their own out of India's body politic." With his harnessing of Indian Muslim's aspirations, Sir Syed "made possible the emergence of Iqbal as the possible leader of Muslim Indians' most cherished hopes and yearnings, and of Jinnah as the political craftsman to ... carve out from that nationalism a territorial abode."

Two-Nation Theory

Many argue that the official two-nation theory—Hindus and Muslims in India being two separate and distinct nations—is now defunct as the separation of East Pakistan from Pakistan in 1971 and the establishment of Bangladesh indicate total repudiation of this theory.[7] In the modern-day world, attempting to unite disparate groups of people into a single nation-state just on the basis of a common religious belief is a nonstarter. Indeed, if it could be done, why would there be fifty-one Muslim states in the OIC, and why would Arabia split into so many states, even though they are all Islamic? The reason is that because the goal of the well-being, prosperity, and common good of a people trumps religious beliefs. However, in the case of Pakistan, the two-nation theory was not a two-religion theory. Jinnah and the Muslim League's founding fathers of Pakistan did not intend to establish a theocratic Islamic state, but rather they envisioned a Muslim welfare state, a state with basic avowed objectives leading to the betterment of the lives of Muslim Indians, especially in the political, economic, and social realms. As Jinnah enunciated in his 1947 landmark address to the new nation, "You are free to go to your temples, you are free to go to your mosques or any other place of worship in this State of Pakistan. You may belong to any religion or caste or creed- that has nothing to do with the business of the State." [8]

Islamist Nationalism

The tide of fundamentalism and Islamist nationalism first emerged in the newly created Pakistan state in 1953 when anti-Ahmadiyya riots took place in Panjab province instigated by the Islamic supremacist party, Jamaat-e- Islami. Prior to that but soon after the death of its founder and first ruler, Mohammad Ali Jinnah, the constituent assembly in 1949 passed the inconsistent Objectives Resolution (discussed in previous chapters), and this later became a part of the preamble of the 1956 constitution. [3] This resolution introduced what is called the ideology of Pakistan, which calls for Islamic principles as well as democratic concepts. This tide reached its full crescendo in 1977 through the dictator General Zia ul Haq, who not only incorporated this objectives resolution into the main articles of the 1973 constitution but also included in its other Islamist provisions. This attempted social and political transformation of the country into a theocratic Islamist state still threatens the vision of a modern Muslim state.

Ethnic Nationalism

Ethnic nationalism, pride and passion for a particular ethnic region, cannot be denied in Pakistan in the four ethnic provinces of the Pakistani state. Of course, it does exist, given the country's four distinct ethnic nationalities—Baloch, Panjabi, Sindhi, and Pashtun. These four ethnicities have their own brand of nationalism as each of them takes pride and inspiration from their separate and unique culture, history, land, language, and norms.

However, ethnic nationalism of a single ethnicity, confined to that specific ethnicity, cannot be stretched to encompass the whole state at a national level. It is not suitable for an ethnically diverse country as Pakistan for a variety of reasons, such as national integration and equality. Dominance in the country of one particular ethnic nationalism, such as Panjabi nationalism, would inevitably result in resentment and national disintegration by other ethnicities. It's the sine qua non of an inclusive nation-state that all its ethnicities and diverse people be treated equally and enjoy equal benefits without discrimination. As nations have found out, inequality along ethnic lines breeds alienation and risk of rebellion. The mistreatment of Chechnya in the big Russian state is a case in point.

Linguistic Nationalism

Linguistic nationalism, much like ethnic nationalist, is based on the prevalence of a single ethnic population of a state speaking a single language. Its prime examples are Germany and Japan. However, like ethnic nationalism, linguistic nationalism is also not feasible for Pakistan state which has diversity of languages and lacks linguistic homogeneity.

Martial Nationalism

With military shows, military parades, national celebrations of military days, and dominance of military news in the media, some wonder if a martial nationalism is the de facto nationalism of Pakistan. Military does indeed play a very important ideological role in the country on a national scale. It's a formidable motivating force for the troubled masses desperately craving any feel-good national accomplishments that would lift up their spirits. While the military can be a source of national pride to many of the citizens, it is also not favorably looked upon in some quarters, especially in smaller provinces. It has this perception because of its unpopular state actions. In any event it cannot be the sole basis of Pakistan's nationalism since the paramount objective for the creation of the country was the prosperity and the well-being of Muslims in this part of the subcontinent. Moreover, a nationalism that's martial or militarized in nature promotes jingoism, xenophobia, and hostility toward other countries and people, not peace or progress. [9]

Pakistani Welfare Nationalism

For more than seventy years, the brand of ideological nationalism imposed on the people of Pakistan by its rulers has by and large failed to provide them their basic needs of safety, security, health, food, shelter, and education for their children. It has failed to unite them as a vibrant nation. Ethnic rebellions in Balochistan, KPK, Sindh, separation of Bangladesh, and alienation of religious minorities is evidence of its failure and destructive effects on national polity. What this country needs are a unifying, dynamic, motivational nationalism with the ultimate goal of providing for the welfare and well-being of all people of the country—progress and prosperity being its cornerstones. And that new nationalism can be termed as the Pakistani welfare nationalism. It will serve as a sustainable glue that holds the diverse country together because people will fight for a state that serves their needs and protects their interests and benefits.

This is an era when pure supremacist and exclusive ideologies are on the wane, when socialist nations are adopting capitalistic ways and vice versa, and where many Muslim nations such as Pakistan are ideologically in between the extremes. We only have to look in the proximity of the Asian neighbors, including China, Singapore, South Korea, Malaysia, and Indonesia, to realize how increasingly prevailing this trend has become. The bottom line is that in the modern social contract between the state and its citizens, the goals of the welfare and well-being of the citizens takes precedence over power considerations of the state. A nationalism based on territorial expansion and revisionism will not evoke as much lasting loyalty and passion for Pakistan state as the one based on a promise to deliver progress and prosperity to the people.

Pakistan's welfare nationalism will not only be the key to national cohesion but will also be instrumental to country's future progress and prosperity as it is based on doing public good and improving the welfare of the people. Its two guiding principles—equal treatment of all citizens of the state and rule in the interests of the nation—would help keep the country on an upward trajectory.[10] Focused on the welfare and prosperity of the citizens, such nationalism would avoid war and hostility with neighbors. Its other fruitful by-products would include the fostering of respect and dignity of the citizens, equality, rule of law, democratic and responsive public institutions, effective governance, and democratic order.

CHAPTER 6
Reforming the Institutions

As in any democratic order, healthy, robust underpinnings of critical institutions are the key to a state's survival and progress. On the other hand, weak, unresponsive, ineffective institutions spell disaster and doom a state, eventually triggering its collapse. Social scientists Dawn Acemoglu and James A. Robinson (*Why Nations Fail?*) classify institutions as "extractive" versus "inclusive" and contend that the former rent-seeking institutions gradually erode the viability of a state. And as societies become more complex and complicated, so do the state's institutions, which in turn call for greater oversight and efforts by the nation to prevent the institutions from becoming tools in the service of power-seeking elite. John Taintey talks about this in his book *The Collapse of Complex Societies—Nations Collapse.*

The story of Pakistan is a story of weak, predatory institutions that were unresponsive and unaccountable to the needs of the people.

A. Strengthen the Legislature

Articles 50-89 of the Pakistan Constitution lays down the composition, powers and functions of the Parliament. [1]

Pakistan's bicameral legislature consists of two houses of the

Parliament or *Majlis- e-Shoora*: the: National Assembly, which is the lower house, and the upper house called the Senate., The National Assembly consists of 272 directly elected seats s plus 70 reserved seats for women and minorities for a five-year term. The Senate has a total of 104 seats for a six-year term of which 23 members are elected by the provincial assemblies on the basis of equal representation of each province plus 8 from FATA and 4 from Federal Capital.

The basic function of the National Assembly is to make laws, elect the Prime Minster and make amendments to the Constitution. The role of the Senate is to pass all bills except the money bills, which is the sole prerogative of the National Assembly, accountability or oversight of the Executive branch and representation of the federating units. [2]

Phase 1

The legislative branch of Pakistan's government is the centerpiece of its parliamentary democracy. It occupies a unique status in the trilogy of the three branches of government in that it's the only one institution that embodies the sovereign of its people manifested through their chosen representatives in the legislature. At present, it's a weak and powerless institution that is easily bypassed, overridden, or ignored. It is not looked upon with deference as it should be in the corridors of power. [3]

It's needless to say, but the legislature needs to be strengthened and streamlined functionally or procedurally in the initial phase and structurally in the next phase. Starting with the first phase, we should provide the national assembly with adequate legal resources and other professional expertise in fulfilling its core function of drafting and preparing legislation on any topic. For example, the Standing Committee of Law and Justice should have access to services of outside legal counsel if need be to draft and finalize bills for enactments without having the need to go to the Ministry of Law for assistance, particularly in the face of an inherent conflict of interest with the executive branch of the government.[4]

Second, there seems to be ample room for improvement in the assembly's performance of its core function as it pertains to debate and discussion of a bill or a national issue. In order to tighten its deliberative process and to make it more focused, some specific measures need to be taken. For instance, time management should be strictly practiced. Each member may be allowed no more than ten minutes of speaking time during the first reading of a bill or discussion of an issue, and the time should be decreased on the subsequent readings of the bill.

Third, in order for the assembly to earn respect from the public and other institutions, it should require all its members to attend at least 75 percent of its days in session, keeping in view its heavy workload. This may sound trivial, but it's important from an image point of view as well. They must dress in a dignified manner. They can wear either the national dress or business suits.[5]

Fourth, its current budgetary and agenda setting processes seems to be haphazard and hurried without the opposition's input or rights. The ruling majority bulldozing the opposition members in this matter must come to an end, and the latter should be allowed to participate fully in these critical processes.[6]

Phase II

It is ironic that even though the Parliament is the most democratic of the institutions, it has been able to successfully pass a substantial number of important legislations (131 bills from 2008–13), including the game-changing Eighteenth Amendment to the Pakistan Constitution for enforcing provincial autonomy and groundbreaking laws that empower women at the workplace. A lot of political instability in the country can be attributed to the fact that though the supremacy of the Parliament is enshrined it is not shown due respect in the democratic dispensation. The legislature is routinely ridden roughshod by both the executive and judicial branches of the government.[7]

Judiciary has sought fit to meddle in the separate power and the internal functions of the parliament, overruling its constitutional actions and even questioning its constitutional authority to amend the constitution. The executive branch is no less guilty when it comes to bypassing or bullying the parliament. The abysmal use of issuing ordinances is a clear usurpation of the exclusive law-making powers of the Parliament. Although parliament is the one institution that is said to represent the voice of the people, this voice has largely been muffled or silenced in Pakistan's history. Reasons for this non-performance are both internal and external. Internally, it has been the parliament's own failure to produce competent, visionary, selfless and dedicated leaders. Externally, repeated direct and indirect authoritarian and power-seeking interventions in the country's democratic order have fragmented the effective functioning of the parliament. For the Legislative branch to succeed it must establish its effectiveness, credentials confidence, assertiveness in its lawmaking functions.

A nation state legitimizes and authorizes the collective rights of its citizens to rule themselves through the lawmaking powers of the parliament. Hence, in the second phase of its reforms if not sooner, parliament has to find the ways and means to stop this encroachment of its powers and to reassert its lawful authority in the scheme of things.

Second, as related to the previously outlined step, the parliament must take appropriate measures to exercise effective oversight over the executive branch and to monitor the enforcement and implementation of country's laws passed by the parliament. One of the most effective tools that the parliament can employ in this connection is the process of holding parliamentary hearings. Through these hearings the parliament can summon and cross-examine witnesses, government functionaries, citizens, and other stakeholders under oath to find out the truth in any matter concerning Pakistan laws. Necessary authority should be given to the parliament to issue subpoenas to summon any witness, and they must also be granted contempt powers.

Third, the parliament should revamp its structure of committees as some of them seem duplicitous and unnecessary. Why do we need a standing committee on Kashmir when there's already a standing committee on Kashmir affairs and Gilgit Baltistan? Similarly, a committee on government assurances in the senate seems redundant when the national assembly also has one on government assurance. So many categories of committees in the senate and national assembly— standing committees, special committees, parliamentary committees, domestic committees, and senate committees—simply adds to confusion and duplication and encourages a lack of accountability.

B. Revamp the Judiciary

Articles 175-212 of the Pakistan Constitution covers the composition, powers and the functioning of the country's Judiciary and the courts.[12]

Superior Judiciary consists of: the Pakistan Supreme Court (17 judges) which is the apex court; High Courts of each four provinces and the Islamabad High Court (Federal Territory; Sharia Court (8 judges including 3 Ulemmas) to determine if a law is repugnant to the injunctions of Islam; Supreme Appellate Court for Gilgit-Baltistan region.

Subordinate Judiciary comprises of: District and Sessions Courts for every district of each province for civil and criminal cases respectively; Additional District and Additional Sessions Courts for each town and city of the four provinces; Civil Courts and Judicial Magistrate Courts, Classes I, II & III for every town and city with limited jurisdictions; [11]

Special Tribunals (18) for various specialty areas such as: Banking Courts, Customs Courts, Income Tax Courts, Family Courts, Labor Courts, Patent Courts, Juvenile Courts, Anti -Terrorism Court under the Anti-Terrorism Act. [12]

National Accounting Bureau (NAB), an autonomous, constitutionally established Federal institution to fight and prosecute public corruption and economic terrorism. NAB was created by a 1999 Presidential Ordinance, subsequently consolidated under Article 270 A of Pakistan.

Phase 1

Reforming the country's judicial system will be a complex undertaking as it involves decades of dysfunction, corrupt and unethical practices, archaic laws and legal procedures, incompetent judges, a backlog of hundreds of thousands of decades-long cases, and so on. In addition to such formidable problems, it will require coordination and input of all three branches of the government.[13]

Of the previously mentioned two segments of the judiciary, the superior judiciary seems to be performing at a functional and decent level, though it suffers from its own set of problems. However, it's the lower subordinate judiciary that is in disarray and on the verge of breaking down. It needs immediate attention, but where do we start? That is the question.

The subordinate judiciary with its duplicitous and confusing court system has some deep structural problems that would entail a lot of effort and time. Perhaps it's better to first focus on easy pickings such as bottlenecks that require practical solutions. First, information technology can be used to make the system more accessible, convenient, speedier, cost-effective, and transparent for the lawyers, their litigant clients, and the judges at the same time.

Judicial processes such as filing complaints, applicants, and motions, scheduling hearings, processing adjournment dates of cases, appearances, and appointments with judicial officers, making payments against court fees and fines, and other functions should be made online on websites with the relevant courts. This would result in lawyers, their clients, and the judges saving much time. Old, time-consuming practice of court payments through revenue stamps and bank pay orders should be replaced by easier and much faster online payments.

As the use of technology becomes more prevalent in the judicial system, legal statements, case files, and documents can be digitalized. Databases of cases can be shared by all the parties. More sophisticated apps can be developed by the available IT-trained youths of Pakistan. All such digitization would dramatically streamline the flow of both civil and criminal cases. Speedy trials, the holy grail of country's system of justice, might actually become a reality.

This online transformation of our judicial system will be facilitated by the ready availability of the large pool of our youthful talent in this field. Besides helping with modernization and improving the judicial system, this measure would provide gainful employment and an opportunity for further training in IT skills to the country's educated youth.

Second, faster movement of files, speedier trials, and quicker dispensation of civil and criminal cases in the lower courts (as well as in the higher courts) will have a profound effect in downsizing the ever burgeoning civil and criminal dockets before the judiciary.

Third, we must remember that the most important aspect of a system of justice is its trust, respect, and confidence in the eyes of the people. This can be accomplished in a variety of ways. Taking appropriate steps toward employing competent, trained men and women of integrity as judges is the primary requisite. To handle the huge workload of the subordinate judiciary in sprawling towns and cities of the country, the woeful understaffing of judges, prosecutors, and court and police personnel must be addressed. Courtrooms and court buildings should be equipped with modern and secure facilities.

Fourth, technological advances in the field of forensics investigations, such as DNA testing, fingerprinting, chemical analysis of evidence, video surveillance, social media evidence, and much more must be deployed. This will not only expedite resolution of cases and removal of doubts concerning burden of proofs and conclusive evidence but also greatly aid in eradicating the insidious practice of false testimonies and lying, hired witnesses that's so prevalent in our current judicial system.

Fifth, during the first phase of transformation of the judicial and legal system, we can start with streamlining civil and criminal procedures. Procedures that result in endless delays in the adjudication of cases must be modified. Deadlines and time lines for various legal and judicial actions, including filing responses and seeking adjournments among others, must be shortened, while antiquated rules requiring unnecessary paper chase, attestations, affidavits, and other documents must be discarded as part of an ongoing process.

The lower or subordinate judiciary provide the roots of the judicial tree. If the roots are strong, the system of justice will flourish. If the roots are weak, the whole judiciary, including the superior judiciary, will wither away.

Phase 2

After tackling some of the basic anomalies and procedural obstacle inherent in the lower judiciary, we can begin to institute necessary improvements in the functioning of the superior judiciary and also make changes in substantive laws. The previously outlined reform measures highlighted for upgrading the lower judicial system, such as the application of technology, are also relevant for the smooth and efficient functioning of the higher court system.

The underlying goal of reforming Pakistan's substantive laws and rules both in the civil and criminal domains must be to replace laws that are archaic, obsolete, and irrelevant with the ones that are modern, responsive, and relevant to our present-day societal needs and compulsions. In an effort to achieve that end, a body or a commission under the auspices of the parliament constituting of members of legal fraternity, judiciary, executive government and people's representatives should be established. The findings and recommendations of such a body for modernizing and streamlining the country's statuary laws must then be discussed and debated in the parliament and enacted eventually and codified.

C. Improve Governance and Bureaucracy

Basic government set-up is as follows. The Federal Government of Pakistan, headed by the Prime Minister as the Chief Executive, comprises of Establishment Division, about 40 Federal Ministries, 12 Directorates, various public companies that include Pakistan Railways, Pakistan International Airlines, various electric, power and gas, and other public companies, regulatory bodies, various autonomous bodies and commissions.[8] The four provincial governments of Sindh, Panjab, Baluchistan and KPK, are headed by their respective Chief Ministers with Chief Secretaries as the chief provincial bureaucrats and consists of provincial ministries drawn from the provincial assemblies. Each province is headed by a Governor who is appointed by the President of Pakistan as the representative of the Federal Government. [9]

Bureaucrats and provincial governments are staffed by the country's elite civil servants (the Central Superior Service cadre), lateral entry consultants on contracts, and hundreds of thousands of subordinate and clerical personnel.

Phase 1

Whenever there's talk of reforming Pakistan's well-entrenched bureaucracy, attention invariably turns to the elite CSS (Central Superior Services) bureaucrats while ignoring the lower tiers of the bureaucratic machinery that far outnumber the CSS officers and the fact that it is these clerks, secretaries, patwaris and other file pushers who are the public face of the government that the people interact with. So, any change or reform of bureaucracy should start with first getting making the functionality of the lower (and larger) bureaucracy right and smooth.

First, we should provide to the clerical and support staff of our government the proper training as how to interact with the public as their tax-paying customers. Second, they must be fully conversant with the rules and regulations of the particular services of their department or organization along with necessary skills and ethics required for their jobs. Third, adequate working conditions, compensation packages, and motivational bonuses should be provided along with job security. Fourth, as much IT should be included in their work as possible (e.g., online filings, digital payments, and record keeping). Online files should replace the paper files many are accustomed to, thereby saving time and money, reducing corruption, and improving efficiency.

Induction of Military Officers

Closely linked with the topics of bureaucracy and civilian-military affairs is the induction of retired and even active officers of the country's armed forces in key or senior management positions in the civil bureaucracy, its various departments and agencies of the government. It's estimated that hundreds of such military offices have been so appointed in strictly civilian roles, ranging from CEOs of government corporation to vice-chancellors of universities and colleges to chairman or members of the Federal and Provincial Civil Service Commissions. In the Ministry of Interior we have the spectacle of these military officers virtually running the entire ministry, from the minister, secretary and downwards, This ministry might as well be made part of the GHQ of the army.

This unsavory practice must be stopped. It's undesirable on many counts. First of all these officers chose a career in the military voluntarily, nobody forced them to do so. No draft in Pakistan. And they spent their entire career and training in the defense service of the country. After their retirement from military why would they start a civilian government career? Of course, any officer is free to take up another career upon retirement, but not with and at the expense of Pakistan civilian government. Secondly, the senior or management positions in the government require certain kind of specific qualifications including experience, skill, training and education which theses officers lack. And if the criteria of on-the-job-training is substituted for qualifications and specific experience and expertise, then that would be a recipe for administrative disaster in the country. It would mean that anyone in Pakistan could be appointed to any position, irrespective of his or her qualifications and professional experience.

Furthermore, it would be unfair to those Pakistanis who have staked their entire life on a career in civil service. It would sap the motivation and destroy the moral of those civil servants affected by the imposition of such military personnel. This improper practice can be curtailed, if not altogether eliminated, by passing appropriate legislation or better still, by a constitutional amendment either by adding a separate clause restricting such appointments in the civilian governments or its agencies or accordingly modifying Article 243 of the Constitution.

Project Management

Pakistan has drastically suffered from the poor management and timely and efficient implementation of various development projects throughout its history. This signal failure in management of projects has hindered country's development and economic progress. Myriads of ill-planned, incomplete, abandoned or low- quality projects are littered all across the country. The country lacks competent professional workforce who are fully trained in the modern science of project management. Hence Pakistan immediately needs to establish a separate, top draw, professional cadre of project managers in the bureaucratic set up.

Project management is the leading science of modern- day development. Project managers, leading a team of diverse experts, plan, initiate, execute, monitor, quality control, implement, complete and close a given project. It involves all processes and the application of technology and software. Project managers are trained and are responsibly for timely and efficient completion of projects and for achieving specific goals and target of the project. The current practice of the government to transfer and deploy various bureaucrats from different departments to manage a new project is not productive. For one thing, there's no sense of team work, and secondly, no required expertise in the science of project management. This cadre of project managers must be selected from the best available talent in the country and given appropriate grade, compensation with job security and independence.

Phase 2

Ever since the advent of Pakistan, almost every government has tried to bring changes in the civil service that would primarily serve to their own political agendas, but as a result, hardly any meaningful reform has taken place. As far back as in 1953, the government of the day issued the Robert Egger Report about structuring the civil service. Then in 1972, the Administrative Reforms Committee submitted its recommendations for change in the bureaucracy. Its most notable one was the idea of inducting external personnel as lateral entry into the government service. The present PTI Government has constituted the "National Commission for Reform" headed by an ex civil servant, Dr Ishrat Hussain. Its proposals for improvement and efficiency of the sprawling government bureaucracy should be discussed, debated by all the stakeholders, including the Parliament, public and civil servants, and accordingly implemented.

Any reconfiguration of the civil service should encompass its depolarization and decentralization to give its officers independence, control, and flexibility in the decision-making process. Second, their compensation and promotion should be based on the merit of their performance, the results achieved, and the competitive pay scale in the marketplace. Third, a unified pay scale might not be feasible for employing experts in specialty occupations such as IT managers or scientists. In the hiring and firing of technocrats and experts, the concerned department or entity should be given greater authority and control. The bottom line is that the leapfrogging advances in information technology, social media, and new frontiers of human society have made the old notion of a generalized bureaucrat serving all or any sector of administration obsolete. These technological advances and innovations have drastically changed the game for governments servants, and they have to adjust or reinvent themselves accordingly.

D. Provide Effective Education

It wouldn't be hyperbole to assert that the state of education in the country is more than alarming: It's desperate as some basic facts indicate. According to the 2017–18 Economic Survey of Pakistan, the rate of literacy in the country is mere 58 percent of the population. That translates into ninety-two million (42 percent) people who cannot read or write. That's an astounding and massive figure. [14] In fact, 46 percent of country's children do not attend primary school. Though the government has tried to bring in reforms in education, the education system remains largely broken and in disarray. The basic reason for the educational disaster is the fact that the governmental bureaucracy—at the federal, provincial, district and local level—is simply not up to the task of administering thousands of government-run schools and the hundreds of boards of education. The government does not possess education management skills, the intellectual capacity, and/or the academic independence to hire and train capable teachers, to draw up modern curricula for children, or to provide the needed resources. The country's most urgent challenge is ensuring that these vast number of children go to school. One of the main reasons for such rampant illiteracy is the pittance that the government spends on education, a mere 2.2 percent of the GDP.

The problem of education or the lack of it is further compounded by an indoctrination curriculum in schools in the name of patriotism and religious supremacism. The result is the production of robotic students deprived of cognitive development and devoid of critical thinking. So, any solution to this crisis in education, which is the country's backbone, should encompass not only building thousands of schools that are adequately equipped and staffed but also the modernization of the curriculums and teaching methods. Pakistan has a critical shortage of skilled workers in all professions. Hence, it must also focus on establishing technical and vocational institutes nationwide.

E. Optimize Military Organization

There's no denying that Pakistan's military is the most organized institution in the country and also the most efficient and results-oriented. Sometimes operating in difficult circumstances, its disciplinary performance in pursuit of its objectives is commendable. However, there are certain areas where some introspection and improvement are required, and such efforts will substantially benefit both the military and the country.[16]

First, the military's acquisition and procurement policies for goods, services, weapons, and systems need to be streamlined, modernized, and made transparent to prevent the recurrence of such procurement scandals as the purchases from France of Agosto 90B submarines and Exocet missiles by Pakistan Navy and purchase from France of Mirage jets by Pakistan Air Force (Refer to Imam R. Sehri's *Judges and Generals in Pakistan*.) [18] Perhaps it can learn from the US military's adoption of acquisition rules and regulations, which are called DFARS (Defense Federal Acquisition Regulation Supplement). Second, deficiencies in command and control structures and the military's decision-making apparatus must be addressed. Investigative journalist Nasim Zehra (*From Kargil to the Coup: Events that Shook Pakistan*) highlighted some operational inadequacies and gaps witnessed in *Kargil* operations.

However, since the military's database is not accessible because of security considerations, only internal members can undertake the improvement of its functionality. [17]

F. Control Corruption

A lot has been said about corruption in Pakistan in a relentless narrative from the state to discredit and demonize politicians and government officials. The incessant drumbeat of corruption has been the go-to propaganda tool by military power grabbers as well as civilian rulers to justify and perpetuate their rule. For political purposes, the level of corruption has been exaggerated to ridiculous heights in amounts of hundreds of billions of dollars when the GDP of the country has been in the $200-400 billion range. In a bid to create a corruption hysteria in the country, the new PTI government went so far as to claim that Pakistanis had illegally transferred more than $200 billion to Swiss and other offshore accounts and unlawfully purchased properties overseas in Dubai, etc., worth another $200 billion.

The Debt Inquiry Commission appointed by PTI Government has just demolished the incessant, corruption bogey or propaganda that previous political rulers "looted" money from loans, debts and monies received by the country. After months- long investigation the Inquiry found that all loans and debts received from 2008 to 2018 were duly deposited in the Government's Account No. 1 and none of the amount was misused or embezzled.(See Ansar Abbasi, The News daily, , November 6, 2019). Similarly, the Chairman of the Federal Bureau of Revenue (FBR), Shabbar Zaidi, has now officially stated that the overseas money transfers and purchase of assets there were not unlawful since they were permitted by Foreign Accounts Ordinance and other laws of Pakistan. Furthermore, such total assets abroad were $5.5 billion rather than hundreds of billions of dollars and the total tax collected on them by the FBR was merely about $31 million. See FBR Report by Masood Haider, The News daily, November 8, 2019. Of course, governmental corruption is a big problem for the country. but it certainly is not the hydra-headed monster that it's made out to be.

Actually, corruption in Pakistan is on a much lower scale than other Asian nations such as China, India, Indonesia, etc., given the small size of Pakistan's economy (GDP). For one thing, these countries have scores of certified billionaires while Pakistan has none.

G. Reform or Disband NAB

To effectively and legally fight corruption in the government National Accountability Bureau (NAB) is not the right vehicle. It's a monstrosity created by country's powerful ruling forces that trashes the human rights and rule of law guaranteed in the Pakistan Constitution. It basically meant to serve a twofold purpose—to eliminate popular and effective political opponents of the current government and to perpetuate the rule of the power brokers. [15]

The NAB's structure and rules are ill-suited to investigate, prosecute, and convict those accused of governmental corruption as per the requirements of due process, law, and the Pakistan Constitution. It is inherently defective in the eyes of the law, especially since its very passage and enactment is legally dubious. Its modus operandi of prosecuting opponents in the name of corruption consists of first raiding the homes and offices of those targeted in order to discover any corruption evidence. If these officials fail to find anything, they either plant incriminating evidence (like it recently planted 25 kilograms of heroin in the car of PMLN leader, Rana Sanaullah) or go ahead with prosecuting and convicting these targets any way on the dubitable charge of "living beyond means."

One-sided persecution of opponents leaves little doubt that the NAB is being used as a political weapon to punish political opponents of government corruption and to silence them. Its practice of conducting quasi judicial hearings and trials and then passing judgments has been legally flawed and often violates the due process rights guaranteed to citizens by the constitution. Economically speaking, it has caused huge national loss on account of the political instability it has created, especially among the potential investors, despite its claims of receiving big amounts from the alleged corrupt through fine and plea bargaining.

Besides targeting political leaders, businessmen, industrialists and entrepreneurs NAB is also abusing its corruption-fighting authority by summoning and arresting and jailing honest civil servants for taking policy decisions in the past years that were required to be taken in the course of their official duties. This has created a climate of harassment, intimidation and fear of midnight knocks at their homes by NAB police forcing the civil servants to stop or delay taking decisions on files for fear of being arrested and punished later. This in turn has adversely affected the smooth functioning of the governmental machinery and the needed good governance. The sad part is that even though there's no corruption involved in these cases against civil servants and no evidence of corrupt behavior, NAB still goes after them with summons and arrests to question the soundness and motivations of the administrative decisions they took years ago, decisions for which they had government immunity. Needless to say, that these persecutions by NAB are unlawful and *ultra vires*.

Almost ever since the inception of Pakistan, the *corruption card* or *corruption bogey* has been regularly used by the powers that be to silence public dissent and to suppress the voices for ethnic rights. In 1949, two years after Pakistan's independence, the country was still without a constitution as it was being ruled under the 1935 Act of India, but the prime minister Liaquat Ali Khan thought fit to remove five chief ministers of Sindh province and seven thousand political workers under a hastily enacted law in 1949, the Public Representatives Disqualification Act (PRODA).

Immediately after grabbing power in 1958, the military dictator General Ayub used a dubious law, specifically the 1959 Elective Bodies Disqualification Act (EBDO), to disqualify three most popular politicians of East Pakistan—Hussain Suhrawardy (a former prime minister), Mujib ur Rehman (who subsequently became a founding father of Bangladesh), and Maulana Bhashani (who espoused the rights of the oppressed Bengalis). Ayub also dismissed the cream of Pakistan's highly ethical CSP civil servants for corruption charges when they were skeptical of his illegal rule.

Subsequently, in 1977, upon assuming power, General Zia ul Haq inserted in the Pakistan Constitution the ambiguous, broad requirement that the members of the parliament must be honest, *sadiq* and *ameen* in order to block political opponents of his brutal regime, a provision that was later used to banish the elected prime minister Nawaz Sharif from political office for life.

Then came General Musharraf's coup, and he turned to the bogey of corruption to justify his shredding of the constitution and seizure of civilian power. In 1999, he established the National Accountability Bureau (NAB), which gave the government draconian authority to fight public corruption and economic terrorism. General Musharraf created the NAB not by a legislative act but by promulgating a presidential ordinance, thus circumventing the constitutional order. It violated the constitution not only in the manner it was enacted but more egregiously, in how it infringed on due process and fundamental rights guaranteed by the constitution. The NAB courts shifted the burden of proof to the accused in the "living beyond means" offense, which itself is too broad and nebulous to pass any constitutional test. In fact, the creation of the NAB was redundant since a proper law to fight corruption, the Ehtesaab Act, already existed at the time of its enactment.

Incidentally, in July of 2019, the London High Court ordered the NAB to pay a penalty in the amount of Rs 5.21 billion to Broadsheet, LLC, a UK-USA–based assets recovery firm, for service in connection with former prime minister Nawaz Sharif's witch hunt.

A better way to fight corruption would be to reform and empower the white-collar crime divisions of the lower and high courts in the judiciary with the necessary legal authority and equip them with adequate human and forensic resources, or we could establish a truly autonomous body that operates within the confines of the law and the constitution in a nonpartisan manner. This would go a long way toward strengthening the justice system in a permanent, nonpartisan, manner. If the NAB's total repeal is not pursued, then it must be revised substantially to satisfy all the requirements of due process rights and the constitution.

H. Strengthen Political Parties.

"Freedom of Association: Every citizen, not being in the service of Pakistan, shall have the right to form or be a member of a political party..."
--- Article 17(2) of the Pakistan Constitution

In Pakistan a citizen's right to establish, organize and operate a political party is guaranteed by the above Article 17(2) of the Constitution, while it is also based on the freedom of speech and expression (Article 19), freedom of assembly (Article 16), and the equal protection clause (Article 25) of the Constitution. Bolstered by these fundamental guarantees of the Constitution, Pakistani political parties are legally not at the mercy of the government's discretions and whims: every institution is obligated to not hinder or undermine the formation or functioning of t political parties.

Pakistan's most prominent political parties are :

1. Pakistan Tehreek -e- Insaaf (PTI)- currently ruling at the center.
2. Pakistan Muslim League- N (PMLN)
3. Pakistan Peoples' Party (PPP)
4. Awami National Party (ANP)
5. Jamiat - e- Ulema Islam- F (JUIF)
6. Jamaat -e -Islami (JI)
7. Pakistan Muslim League- Q (PMLQ)
8. Muttahida Qaumi Movement (MQM)
9. Balochistan National Party (BNP)
10. Pakistan Awami Tehreek (PAT)
11. Pakistan Sarzameen Party (PSP)

Political parties are the lynchpin of a democratic, representative political order. It's inconceivable to have a representative government without political parties. They link people with the government of a country, serves as a watchdog of government's actions and governance, provide elected representatives to the parliament, provide personnel for cabinet and governance, serves as conduit to people's aspirations. And most importantly, political parties in a democratic set up are supposed to serve as a bulwark against dictatorial rule and tyranny over people, keeping alight the flame of democracy and freedom and the will of the people. Because of such crucial role they are required to play, it is imperative that political parties are robust, strong and vigilant. Be that as it may, Pakistan's own experience with political parties has been far from satisfactory; in fact, it has been quite disappointing.

By and large political parties in Pakistan have been weak, ineffective, feudal, dynastic, fragmented, power hungry, corrupt and undemocratic- much like the rest of the country. But in all fairness, politicians alone are not to blame for their mess. Governments, non-political rulers and other institutions of the country must share the blame. For one thing, how can the pollical parties be solely blamed when for about half the period of country's existence, they were denied any say in Pakistan's political affairs or denied any opportunity to share power in the government and rule. For more than thirty years, political parties were systematically disenfranchised and dis-empowered.

Consequently, a lot of burden to strengthen political parties, make them stronger, effective, responsive and transparent rests on the shoulders of authorities and other institutions of the country. They must be encouraged to be open and transparent in their internal structures and processes. Periodic seminars for political parties should be conducted where they are educated by experts in the workings of a modern political party. They must be instructed in account keepings and ancillary financial matters. Election Commission of Pakistan, for instance, could play a constructive role in improvements within political parties. They must be told that democracy, like charity, begins at home, within their own organizations first, by a fair election of their office bearers. Government, judiciary and other institutions must treat their office holders with respect and dignity. Respecting and strengthening political parties mean establishing the norms and political traditions of the country's democracy that are se vital for the growth and sustainability of democracy itself.

CHAPTER 7

Fighting Terrorism and Extremism

Fighting Terrorism

Pakistan has shown renewed determination in tackling terrorism through its various antiterror institutions. Recently, the Pakistan Army's chief general Qamar Jawaid Bajwa, using the platform of 220 Corps Commanders meeting at GHQ, made a strong statement when he said, "Having achieved stability against terrorism, Pakistan is on positive trajectory of becoming a state where prerogative of use of weapons rests with the state alone and socio-economic development is taking preeminence." The army resolved to fully support the implementation of the 2015 National Action Plan (NAP) in fighting terrorism and extremism in the country and to support all stakeholders in this struggle.[1]

The cold blooded massacre of 145 school children along with 6 teachers in class rooms of the Army Public School located in the north west city of Peshawar, Pakistan, on December 16, 2014, by terrorists belonging to Tehreek- e- Taliban (TTP) was a watershed moment in the country's blood-laced history of terrorism and jihadism—a war that has claimed a total of estimated 60,000 lives within Pakistan.[2] As a result of the nationwide shock and anger at this infamous slaughter of schoolchildren, the country's parliament swung into action and passed the National Action Plan (NAP) in June 2015 pursuant to the National Counter Terrorism Authority (NACTA), which was previously established in 2013. Under Article 4 of NACTA, NAP was given the main task to "develop active plans against terrorism and extremism" and combat whatever finances terrorism.[3] The organization was to undertake the implementation at the earliest time. In the fight against terrorism and terror funding, NAP had a twenty-point agenda, including the establishment of special military courts for expedited trials of accused terrorists, a ban on the glorification of terrorist organizations in the media, and a prohibition of extremist, intolerant publications and their distribution in the country.[4]

Pakistan's counterterrorism efforts were effectively started in 1997 with the passage of Anti-Terrorism Act (ATA) by the national assembly, which provided the death penalty for crimes of terrorism and any act done for the benefit of a proscribed organization.[5] In the wake of the bloody February 14, 2019, *Pulwama* terror attack in the Indian side of the disputed Kashmir state, in which forty-seven Indian troops were blown to pieces by suicide bombings believed to be carried out by Pakistan-based Jaish- e- Mohammad group, such efforts by Pakistan have found new urgency as pressure from the international community has mounted.[6] In 2018, the Paris-based Financial Action Task Force (FATF) placed Pakistan on its *gray list* of countries failing to stop money laundering and terror financing by designated terror groups. If the country is unable to satisfy FATF in this regard by September of 2019, it then faces the risk of being placed on the *black list*, a step that would have disastrous consequences for securing credit and financing from international institutions and banks.

Recently, NACTA banned sixty-nine terror outfits in the country, matching the terror lists of the US State Department and that of the United Nations. Among the most notorious and lethal terror or jihadi organizations are Jaish- e- Mohammad (JeM0), Lashkar -e- Tayyaba (LeT), Jamaat- ud- Dawa (JuD), Tehreik -e -Taliban (TTP), Haqqani Network (HN), Al-Qaeda (AQ), Lashkar -e- Jhangvi (LeJ), and

Sipah- e-Sahaba (SSP). And on July 13, 2019, Pakistan's counterterrorism department charged the internationally designated LeT leader, Hafiz Saeed, mastermind of the *Mumbai* terror attacks in India (November 26–29, 2008) that resulted in the deaths of about 166 civilians, including Americans, and twelve other key members of this group under the Anti-Terrorism Act for money laundering and terror funding. [7]

Military Operations

The Pakistan Army deserves credit for launching a series of effective military operations in its fight against Islamist terrorism in its northwestern territories. Most noteworthy among them were the Zarb- e -Azb and Rah- e- Haq operations. Operation Zarb-Azb 2014 was launched in 2014 in the North Waziristan tribal agency to target hideouts, command structures, and sanctuaries of terror outfits that included TP (Tehrik -e- Taliban Pakistan), LeJ (Lashkar e Jhangvi), and Al-Qaeda. This operation involved division-size formation and air force jets. It was largely successful in destroying sanctuaries, command centers, and supply lines of these outfits. The second most important military operation, Rah-e-Haq, was started in 2007. Three phases were launched against the near occupation of Swat Valley in the KPK province, not far from the capital city of Islamabad, and these were meant to wipe out the TNSM and associated terror groups. This operation was conducted by army battalions with cavalry, artillery, and air support. It was successful to a large extent in dislodging these mullah terrorists from Swat, culminating in operation Rah- e- Nijat to clear out remnants of these groups.

Other operations conducted against the jihadi terrorists were the operation Sher- e -Dil in 2008 in Bajaur tribal agency and the 2011 operation Kuh-e-Sufai in the Kurram Agency. Finally, in 2017, operation Radd-ul- Fassad was launched to eradicate terror cells in the country and to consolidate gains of the earlier counterterrorism operations. However, it would be hyperbolic to contend that terrorism has been completely eliminated from Pakistan, though its fury and full force have been confronted and blunted both in terms of lives lost (about sixty thousand) and resources spent. This destructive scourge is still alive and kicking, and we can gauge its presence by recent lethal terror attacks in Lahore, KPK, Karachi, Balochistan, and the cities of Gwadar, Quetta, Chaman, etc. This existential threat to the state must be fought relentlessly with resolute determination both in the border regions and in the urban cities.

Crucial Second Front

Triumph over terrorism involves militarily defeating the Taliban/jihadi enemy on all battlefield fronts without settling for a stalemate. That is a prerequisite to Pakistan's survival, the state's existential validity, the country's progress, and the people's prosperity.

It's despairing to know that a comprehensive, crucial victory over terrorism is still nowhere in sight. As events in the not too distant past indicated that the enemy was inflicting some heavy blows in Pakistan's mainland, the second front of their declared war against the country. From Quetta to Gilgit-Baltistan, from Peshawar to Karachi, the enemy was attacking ruthlessly, causing immense damage to life, property, morality, and the image of the country.

Broadly speaking, the Taliban and jihad groups in their war against the state and people of Pakistan have attacked on two separate fronts as part of their strategy. The first front in the northwest tribal areas, and the second is in the mainland, the heart of the country, with the humungous urban and rural areas.

In the first front, our armed forces are confronting the enemy, sacrificing the lives of its soldiers, though fighting the enemy in a haphazard, piecemeal manner without a grand strategy for annihilation of the enemy and for victory. Still, the army has been partially successful in eliminating thousands of enemy combatants and defeating the enemy in quite a few operations.

However, in the second battlefield front, namely our cities and villages, the army has even failed to show up to defend and fight the bloodthirsty enemy, giving them free reign and open field to attack, bomb, kill, and destroy at will.

This vast front of urban and rural areas inhabited by the majority of Pakistan's 180 million unarmed people presents an almost illimitable number of soft targets (targets that are virtually indefensible by civilian law enforcement agencies). How many people, how many homes, how many mosques, how many shopping centers, how many schools and hospitals, how many streets and building and structures can be successfully defended with trained and fully armed police or security guards around the clock? Not many.

The enemy can literally pick and choose from the endless array or a smorgasbord of vulnerable targets in our city streets and village pathways. It's no surprise then as to how and why the Taliban/jihadi enemy has been so hugely successful in this civilian front, inflicting the majority of civilian casualties here, estimated to be about forty thousand out of the total estimated forty-eight thousand people killed, including our soldiers. In addition, these attacks and bloody onslaughts have devastated the country's economy, hurt businesses and investment, harmed the game of cricket, our national pastime, and all in all, created a climate of paralyzing fear and intimidation throughout the country, crushing the national spirit and shredding to pieces the writ of the state.

As is obvious from the previously outlined, it is this countrywide second front with all its infrastructure and population base that is of more critical importance for the viability and the very continuity of the state than even the primary border front.

It is a fundamental principle of war strategy: In order to prevail over your enemy, you have to defeat the enemy in all the battlefield fronts. To achieve victory on one front and to ignore and be devastated in another will not vanquish your enemy. At best, a selective approach will only serve to prolong the war. At worst, it will make enemy stronger and more unyielding.

If engaging with the enemy on the second front is as critical as combating the enemy in the first front, then an appropriate strategy must be tailored to effectively fight, eliminate, and subdue the Talban/jihadi syndicate in the battlefield of cities and villages as well. Full collaboration with the police and the army (and all the law enforcement agencies) as well as with the citizens will be essential in this endeavor.

Since the enemy has infiltrated various segments of our society and has established a vast network of agents, informants, suppliers, supporters, and other enablers inside our borders, then at least a two-prong strategy should be employed by the armed forces.

First, all agents, infiltrators, supporters, suppliers, and others who work with the enemy and who are embedded within the police, law enforcement, intelligence agencies, the armed forces itself, the bureaucracy, the media, academia, the madrassas, and civil society must be identified, purged, and effectively disabled.

Second, all the hardcore militants all across the cities and villages must be targeted and eliminated, and their base structures and hideouts must be attacked and destroyed. Such a massive offensive with the possibility of bloodshed and violence on an unprecedented scale may seem to be a tall order, and of course, it's easier said than done. But in the face of the horrific alternative, what other choices do we have if we don't try to defeat this enemy by any means necessary? Terrorism is just one tactic among others that's employed by the Taliban/jihadist groups in their war against the state and people of Pakistan. .

People talk about elimination of terrorism in our mainland, which is fine, but terrorism is not an automatic machine that can stop by itself just by condemning or censuring it. As stated previously, terrorism is simply a tactic employed by our inhuman enemy. To stop or eliminate the use of this tactic or method of terrorism, you have to physically disable and militarily defeat the enemy on both fronts of the battlefield.

Verbally persuading this relentless enemy to abstain from committing terrorism in our land has not and will not work unless the enemy is on the verge of being defeated and wiped out. As long as the enemy goes virtually unchallenged and as long as its use of terrorism in the second front is an unmitigated success, it will inexorably continue to employ the tactic of terrorism. And to defeat the enemy in all the fronts, especially in the second front, a defensive strategy will face as is becoming increasingly evident given the formidable magnitude of the region and the seemingly limitless list of soft, vulnerable targets to defend with the limited resources of our country.

Absent an all-out offensive, the miasma of terrorism will continue to shock and bleed us daily with the news of devastating attacks, each more horrifying and audacious than the previous one. To those who say that we shouldn't commit the bulk of the army to go full throttle against this vicious and bloodthirsty enemy or that we should instead save the army, my response is this: Save the army for what? To defend the eastern border against India? But what if there's no country left to defend if we ever have a war with India? And what if the Taliban/jihadi groups outflank it from north to south and encircle it while it continues to sit in its bases as the country around it burns in flames?

This enemy has killed or wounded tens of thousands of our people and inflicted immeasurable destruction of our country in all aspects. If the army cannot or will not defend our nation from this menace now, then who will? The time to fulfill its sworn duty is now.

Fighting Extremism

The underlying incubator of terrorism is the radical mind-set or extremist thinking. Terrorism is simply its outward physical manifestation. Consequently, in order to eliminate terrorism and terrorist groups in Pakistan, this extremist mind-set must first be eradicated. Such a mind-set is developed and nurtured in citizens, mostly young and a few middle-aged people, in such settings as madrassas and primary schools. Other nonviolent Islamist organization such as Ahle Hadith and Tablighi Jamaat, their members numbering in the hundreds of thousand, are composed of mostly poor and gullible citizens in both urban and rural areas, and these groups are huge cesspools for recruitment by jihadi or terror organizations. It's a big mistake to let these organizations operate with impunity and to do as they please just because they profess to be "nonviolent and peaceful." In actual practice they are also the factories for churning out violent fanatics, and their role in promoting terrorism is as sinister as the militant jihadi entities. They must be checked and confronted.

In addition to the private entities, many public organizations in the country must share responsibility for enabling extremist tendencies in the media, society, and its body politic. Indeed, the state has institutionalized intolerance and supremacism, the two factors of extremism, in the Pakistan Constitution and laws that deny superior offices and benefits to non-Muslim citizens. It goes without saying that if the nation is serious about eviscerating extremism in the country, it must discard such provisions.

To wipe out terrorism from the land, Pakistan must fight and banish the roots of the ideology of extremism that have flourished longer than terrorism itself. The battle for the hearts and minds of the Pakistanis must be fought not only at the governmental level but also at the civil society or community level. Fighting an extremist mind-set in an obsessed miasma embraces a wide spectrum of measures ranging from modernizing the environment (chapter 7) to reforming institutions and upgrade education (chapter 6) to changing state policy (chapter 11).

Governmental interventions aside, the civil society and the young generation must be given space in the public arena and encouraged to speak out, analyze, blog, and talk in the media about the destructive effects of extremism, intolerance, and hate. We must encourage youth to hold public events, play sports, and participate in cultural activities that all serves as antidotes to extremist ideas. With the rapid increase in the country's radicalized youth their deradicalization and rehabilitation in the mainstream society assumes critical importance.

In this regard, the government must empower the condign elements of the Muslim population, especially the millennials, who are more likely to serve as catalysts for religious reforms.

Actions by the federal and provincial governments of the country to stop the rising tide of extremist thinking should start at the media, particularly digital media. Pakistan's TV channels tend to advance a somewhat religious supremacist and intolerant viewpoint in express or subliminal ways. Their programming starts with religion and ends with religion, and it's only interspersed by "breaking news" and panel discussions on domestic politics. To be fair, the content of their programming is dictated by PEMRA (Pakistan Electronic Media Regulatory Agency), which ensures that the state narrative is loyally projected and imposed on the nation. Any deviation is immediately reprimanded and punished, and their broadcasts are halted.

Given this context, Pakistan's government's intervention is an attempt to reform the nation's thirty-three odd madrasas or religious schools, which often serve as incubators for jihadi warriors. The government does this by modifying the schools' singular religious curricula and shifts it to lessons along the lines of regular primary schools, monitoring their activities and requiring them to be certified as well. These are well-intentioned efforts, but it's doubtful that this practice will produce the desired end result. Perhaps a better alternative would be to replace these madrasas with government primary schools.

Stopping Destructive Narratives

Jihadi extremist organizations and their proponents in Pakistan take support and strength not only from selected Islamist narratives of history that focus on grievances and the victimization of Muslims but also from government narratives that promotes religious paranoia, hysteria, and supremist tendencies. Of course, some of this official dystopian narrative as seen on TV, in print media, and in government statements and actions is not entirely due to its ideological motivations but fueled by political considerations, serving as a diversion from the people's sufferings and the government's own shortcomings in delivering promised services. Though such destructive narrative is not limited to the government sources, segments of the civil society in both urban and rural areas of the country pick up this thread, creating a climate receptive to extremist ideas. The government and political leaders have to take a bold stand against this unintended but lethal promotion of the extremist mind-set among the citizens.

CHAPTER 8
Strategizing the Economy

Dwarf Economy

As noted previously, Pakistan has a disproportionately inadequate (Gross Domestic Product (GDP) for a nation of about 220 million people. Thus, its fundamental economic challenge for the nation is not corruption (though that's a big problem) or digging out past offenders but rather the push to increase its economic pie and to find the ways and means to achieve this goal through business activities and national productivity, creating markets, attracting investment and capital for much-needed infrastructure, adopting an overarching economic strategy and planning, and other measures enumerated in this chapter and elsewhere in this book. [9]

Broad Economic Strategy

Pakistan is an economically deprived and one of the least developed nations in the otherwise bustling and booming Asian region. [7]. We need serious introspection to determine why this is so. [3] It goes without saying that economic development and accelerated growth are the keys to Pakistan's progress and prosperity.[2] We can best accomplish this or at least start to do so by having a benevolently guided market economy that is not a free-for-all, capitalistic, laissez-faire system or a centralized, controlled, closed national order. Critical ingredients for transforming the economy into a positive, dynamic engine of growth and prosperity should include the measures enumerated in this chapter. As part of the process of strategizing about Pakistan's economy, these measures may be classified into two categories—the immediately achievable and long-term measures. [3]

Immediately Achievable Measures

The process of economic transformation can begin by first implementing the most expedient, low-cost measures that can be easily attainable without requiring huge expenditures, resources, and time commitments. Basically, these include providing economic freedom to all the stakeholders, reforming the institutions, especially governance [8], streamlining and reducing redundant and unnecessary governmental regulations (see chapter 6,), improving Pakistan's Constitution (see chapter 4), and retuning national foreign and security policies (see chapter 10), modernizing and rationalizing the societal and living environment (chapter 9). Unlike the long-term structural changes that require a commitment of formidable will, resources, time, and planning, these fast-track steps would just need political will, committee meetings, and some paperwork. On the other hand, the impact on the national economy that these fast track changes would bring would be tremendous in terms of encouraging foreign and domestic investment, augmenting business activity, and saving huge expenditures relating to defense and security—money that can then be applied to social and education programs. [4]

Long-Term Structural Measures

Development of Pakistani Economic Model

Pakistan has to develop and maintain its own model for economic growth and prosperity based on its own demographics, geography, ethos, and environment. Simply cutting and pasting sections of successful models such as those of China, Sweden, Malaysia, or Singapore would not work since all these models pertain to the unique national characteristics and experiences of each nation. However, certain aspects of their egalitarian economic models may very well be solicited and adopted.

For instance, Pakistan may well take heed from some of the fundamental lessons learned and applied by China in its miraculous economic rise within the global economy. According to noted China expert Professor Susan L. Shirk, the three factors that guided China were avoiding splits in its political leadership, avoiding large-scale social and ethnic unrest and/or uprisings in the country, and maintaining an economic symbiosis with its major trading partners. [1] Unfortunately, Pakistan has failed to uphold each one of these key imperatives for economic progress. Country's political history has been characterized by deep-rooted, sustained infighting among political leaders and rulers, cataclysmic ethnic unrests in the three out of four its provinces, that threatens to morph into existential uprisings at any time, and lack of fostering mutually beneficial trading ties with major economies of the Asian region and the world.

Incremental Industrial Development

Ultimate transformation of the nation from a partially agrarian society to an industrial one must be the focal point for the success of the Pakistani model. Besides the economic edge that industrialized nations enjoy in the international marketplace,[5] Pakistan would be able to gainfully employ and utilize its ballooning youth population in manufacturing nationwide. However, this journey to full industrialization, as the reputable economist Yi Wen and others caution, has to be gradual. Pakistan is not completely devoid of industrialization and infrastructure.[10]. It possesses a substantial share of these resources. Rather than leaping toward high-tech, advanced, capital-intensive industries of electric cars and cutting-edge electronics, the country should try to develop and install midlevel types of industries. As Yi Wen admonishes, "A nation must go through various stages for industrialization. Development is a sequential process of market creation." [6] All the industrialized nations, including Japan, China, and the United States, have gone through this sequential process. Thus, Pakistan has to gradually build the "foundations of a modern industrial state" that include basic to medium industrialization, physical and organizational infrastructure, and markets for its products. To realize these goals, we need visionary leadership, political stability, effective rule of law, an encouraging investment climate, and a modern environment and norms.

Institutions, Infrastructure, and Industrialization

Pakistan's economic progress and prosperity requires responsive state institutions (see the chapter on institutions), adequate infrastructure and sustainable, and sequential industrialization. Its best development phase occurred in the 1960s when it created synergic institutions like PIDC and PICIC as well as NIT to establish and finance new industries. However, the transformation of the nation into an industrialized must be a gradual process. As renowned development economist Yi Wen puts it, "Development is a sequential process of market creation." [10] Pakistan is currently beyond the basic industrialization stage. During the next step, we should establish midlevel industries and manufacturing that can take advantage of our human resources rather than wasting our efforts and precious capital in advance industries. The industrial priority should be to build labor-intensive manufacturing units, and that will provide employment to the surplus of youth while producing cost-competitive items.

Its economic policies should aim for increasing productivity in all spheres and expanding its exports while encouraging the import of various items within the country. As far as the needed infrastructure is concerned, total reliance on CPEC projects is not enough. We will need local initiatives and drives with foreign collaboration for such necessary infrastructure (e.g., Karachi's Metro Train.

Capital and Investment

In order to attract foreign (and domestic) capital and entrepreneurs, cash-starved Pakistan must create a suitable investment climate for doing business in the country. That includes a safe and secure environment, minimum governmental interference and regulations, a long-term finance and tax regime, and a dependable, neutral, transparent legal system that will enforce and honor contracts and political stability.

Honor International Contracts

Pakistan has suffered substantial economic losses in a series of adverse judgments against it by international arbitration tribunals in cases involving breach of contracts entered into by the Pakistan government with foreign companies. *Reko Diq* is the latest case in which the arbitration court, specifically the International Center for Settlement of Investment Disputes (ICSID), awarded a whopping $5.6 billion in damages to an Australia-based multinational called TCC for breach of joint venture agreement to mine gold and copper deposits in the Reko Diq area of Balochistan province. Earlier, on August 22, 2017, ICSID held Pakistan liable to pay about $800 billion in damages for expropriating its assets in violation of a binding joint venture agreement to a Turkish entity called *Karkey Karadenz Electrik Uterim*, which had rented two power-generating boats to Pakistan. Similarly, another arbitration by the International Chamber of Commerce (ICC) has held Pakistan liable for breach of its power-related agreements with international power producers (IPPs). [11]

If Pakistan is serious about stopping such needless economic bleeding, it must pay full attention and adequately comprehend the terms and conditions of international contracts and their binding nature before entering into such agreements. Domestic politics should play zero role in these strictly commercial ventures.

If you drive around the country on its highways and byways, you are bound to come across some sights that are painful to the eyes—unfinished buildings, incomplete structures, and abandoned roads, bridges, dams, power plants, and projects of various types.

Such concrete manifestations of broken promises, breached agreements, and dishonored contracts litter our national landscape from north to south and east to west. The story of Pakistan is a story of these gaping and gashing economic and psychological wounds that have been self-inflicted on the nation by the abrupt cancelation of various project contracts simultaneously accompanied by the stoppage of work thereafter. And none of these breached agreements and dishonored contracts have had more of a devastating impact on the national economy and national reputation than contractual disputes involving international parties.

The country has been witnessing, though somewhat incuriously, a cascade of adverse arbitration decisions against Pakistan by international arbitration forums, including the International Court for Settlement of Investment Disputes (ICSID), the International Chamber of Commerce (ICC), or the United Nations Commission on International Trade Law (UNCITRL), all of which are noted for their neutrality and expertise in cases of international contracts between nations and foreign investors.

Jolted by the unpleasing reality of this fiasco, many of our fellow citizens are asking the inevitable question: Why is Pakistan losing all its international arbitrations cases? There's no mystery to that. There are no rapacious capitalists lurking in the background and no international conspiracies against Pakistan. The answer is simple.

The country is losing because in the eyes of neutral judges, our government and its agencies are not fulfilling their obligations or duties under these agreements and/or violating the relevant bilateral treaty that protects foreign interments. In other words, we are not honoring contracts that we have agreed to and signed.

For instance, in the *Reko Diq* mining case, the International Center for Solution of Investment Disputes (ICSID) arbitrators ruled that the

Pakistan government was in breach of the joint venture contract and the pertinent bilateral investment treaty because it refused to grant TCC, the Argentina-Australia company, the required mining production lease. In the independent power producers (IPPs) case filed by nine IPPs (all domestic) before the International Chamber of Commerce's (ICC) arbitration tribunal in London, all the neutral arbitrators held our federal government violated its agreement as it was in default of its payment obligations to the IPPs.

In order to avoid huge setbacks in international arbitration and to encourage foreign investment, the Pakistan government and its agencies must follow at least some of the following crucial caveats before executing any international or domestic contracts.

First, the government functionaries must closely read, fully comprehend, and agree to all our obligations in the proposed contract, realizing that once it's signed, all its terms and conditions will be enforceable with the force of law.

Second, they must pay close attention to the dispute resolution clauses and fully comprehend the legally binding nature of arbitration and the exclusive jurisdiction of the selected arbitration forum (CSID, ICC, etc.).

Third, the government should be aware that failure to meet our obligations and duties on any pretext can have disastrous consequences and result in payment of billions of dollars in damages.

Fourth, not honoring international contracts tarnishes the country's image as a desirable and trustworthy destination for Sorley needed foreign capital and know-how and also increases political risk coverage and the total cost of doing business in Pakistan. Aside from all legalistic mumbo jumbo, abiding by contracts is also a moral and ethical matter. Since we as Pakistanis have given our word or *zaman* to someone, we must keep our word and honor.

Fifth, we must realize that collateral defense of fraud and corruption in the procurements of international contracts is very difficult to prove since it requires solid documentary proof of its prevalence. With world focus on transparency in international dealings, the US Federal Corrupt

Practices Act and the UK Anti-Bribery Law monitor and punish MNCs for any shady, under-the-table dealings.

Sixth, as we all know that any international contract or joint venture awarded in secrecy gives rise to suspicion of impropriety and corruption, it behooves the government to display transparency in the execution of contracts not only to silence the whispers but also to seek consensus of all stakeholders. Prime examples of such surreptitiously executed contracts are the Qatar LNG Gas Sales and other ancillary agreements whose exact long-term liability exposure is hidden from the people.

Wealth Creation

Perhaps Pakistan's foremost focus in this respect should be the creation of more wealth in the nation, the sum total of goods and services, given the small size of its economy, which doesn't do justice to its big population of 220 million people. It needs accelerated business activities to spur the growth of their gross domestic product (GDP). Facilitation and encouragement of entrepreneurship, innovation, new business ideas and business services must be national objectives.

Tackling Poverty and Inequality

There is no question that the country's egregious levels of poverty and concomitant inequality in living standards are unsustainable for the continued viability of the state. In his book *Enlightenment Now*, Steven Pinker asserts, "The starting point for understanding inequality in the cause of human progress is to recognize that income inequality is NOT a fundamental component of well-being," unlike health, safety, property, and knowledge. Along with economic growth, Pakistan must take transparent steps to reduce the heavy burden of this debilitating inequality among citizens.

In order to alleviate Pakistan's vicious, ever-deepening cycle of poverty, the rate of growth of the national economy must be increased. Emphasizing the critical role played by decreasing inequality in addressing poverty, economist Dr. Kaiser Bengali points out, "Increasing GDP by 1% reduces poverty by 3.6% in the country, but 1% decrease in inequality reduces poverty by 8.5%" (see *Pakistan's Casino Economy*). [7]

Energy Solutions

Energy-its adequate supply and affordable price—is one of the key factors for the development and economy of the country and prosperity of its people. In view of Pakistan's fastest growing population and inevitable energy demands, its not hyperbolic to assert that without necessary availability of energy the nation would not able to overcome its many challenges. True that various Pakistani governments have been making some serious efforts to harness the country's energy resources, including hydrocarbon, hydel, coal resources. However, these efforts have been undertaken in a haphazard manner and without a lot of coordination and vision. The result is that the country still suffers from energy shortage crisis.

As far as exploiting petroleum resources is concerned, credit must be given to various Pakistani administrations for progressively formalizing the country's petroleum policies since 1994, with each policy a refinement on the previous one. The latest policy, the 2012 Petroleum Policy is definitely an attractive one for investors in this risky business, offering more incentives to foreign petroleum companies. Under this Policy, in March 2019 the Pakistan Government awarded a petroleum concession to Kuwait Foreign Petroleum Exploration Company for the Panjab block of *Makhel* for drilling at least one exploratory well besides conducting seismic survey.

However, serious obstacles still remain in its diligent implementation. The countries Revenue and Excise and Tax departments and security agencies have to be brought in line with the guarantees provided in the Petroleum Policy to facilitate the concession holders in their operations. For instance, even though some concession agreements have been awarded and signed with oil and gas companies through competitive and transparent bidding of blocks, they cannot commence exploration on about 23 onshore blocks since the Ministry of Defense is yet to give the required No Objection Certificates (NOCs) for these blocks to commence operations. As to why NOCS are needed from the Defense Ministry is another question that needs to be answered. Its unprecedented as to why the military has the power to interference and veto commercial drilling operations. The delay in starting exploration and drilling may result in substantial losses for the nation as it mat delay production and availability of oil and gas from these concession areas.

The 2012 Petroleum Policy has established three onshore and one offshore licensing zones in order of their hydrocarbon prospectivity, exploration risks factor and the minimum investment required. The three zones are : Zone 1 for West Balochistan, *Pashin*, and *Potowar* basins; Zone II for *Kirthar*, East Balochistan, Panjab, platoform, and Suleman basins; Zone III for the Lower Indus basin. Creation of a new high risk zone for frontier areas, and offering of additional incentives in payment structures and removal of some bureaucratic hurdles are being planned. The Petroleum Policy lays out standard, model Petroleum Concession Agreement (PCA) for onshore exploration, and a model Production Sharing Agreement (PSA) for offshore blocks. The Policy details the Regulatory Process, the Fiscal Regime and various obligations of both the government and the petroleum companies.

The Petroleum Policy professes noteworthy objectives in its mission statement:" To accelerate Exploration and Production activities in Pakistan with a view to achieve maximum oil and gas sufficiency in energy by increasing oil and gas production." Noble goals indeed. But it seems the government lost focus of its intent " to accelerate Exploration and Production activities" when it apparently abandoned its key exploration drive within the country and went for the import of ready-made, expensive liquefied natural gas (LNG). There's seismic and geological data which indicates that some areas of Balochistan (*Kohlu, Zamardan, Bugti* blocks etc) and elsewhere in the country have substantial natural gas reservoirs.

Of course, LNG is a very convenient, off- the- shelf gas, but it's a luxury energy item that rich countries like Japan, China or European nation can afford. For a cash- strapped nation like Pakistan, its import is a big burden on its dwindling dollar reserves. Additionally, to rely on imported LNG is a risky business for security considerations. In the event of any conflict in the region the shipping lanes of LNG could be disrupted. On the other hand, exploration and production of domestic gas would immensely benefit Pakistan and especially Balochistan province in more ways than one. It would, of course, save precious billions of dollars in foreign exchange, increase revenues for the Federal and Balochistan government to be utilized for the welfare of the people, create much needed for unemployed Balochi youth, imbibe national cohesion, develop infrastructure and bring skills, training and technology. Most of all prioritized domestic exploration would foster national energy security, eliminate risk of supply disruption and ensure energy independence for the country in the long term.

Currently the country produces an aggregate of about 95,000 bpd while its total requirements is about 400,000 barrels of oil per day. Pakistan's natural gas production that peaked in 2012 with production of 4.2 billion cubic feet per day (bcfd) is steadily declining with the result that now the gas shortfall is about 2 bfc. Country's huge demand for imported oil and gas magnifies the urgent need for doubling or tripling exploration for oil and gas within the country. The presence of recently discovered huge reservoirs of shale oil and gas in the country should spur the national effort for domestic exploration. After all the government must remember its pledge to the nation in the vision statement of its Ministry of Petroleum and Natural Resources: " To ensure availability and security of sustainable supply of oil and gas, and to coordinate development of natural resources of energy and minerals." For the country to progress, develop and move forward, the necessary hard work and dedication by the government functionaries for energy independence cannot be overemphasized. Energy demand by an burgeoning population and the chronic shortage of energy supply constitutes a national crisis for the country and the government must treat it as such.

Regarding the supply of sustainable and consistent and affordable electric power and energy Pakistan has long way to go even with some concerted efforts to develop the crucial energy sector. It has always been a question of supply and demand of energy. The demand inevitably keeps increasing given the rapidly increasing population and as more development and industrialization increases. A promising development in this respect is the government's seemingly new focus on renewable energy resources. Pursuant to the 2019 draft of country's first Renewable Energy Policy an Alternate Energy Policy Development Board is envisaged to be set up with an ambitious target of producing 30% of country's total power generation through renewable sources by the year 2030. Renewable energy would utilize wind, solar, small hydel and biomass systems. These efforts must continue seriously and with determination as renewable energy can significantly mitigate the energy problem, both from an economic and climate control point of view. In this connection it would be pertinent to mention that about 81% of energy is produced through expensive oil and gas fuel that costs about $ 10 billion annually to the nation. Renewable energy will lessen this huge financial burden of imported fuel.

The energy crisis with its perennial shortages and power outages have continued unabated during the three decades or so greatly disrupting the economic productivity and social life of the nation. It is creditable that power capacity of the country has been increased to about 33,000 MW by 2019 through the construction of various power plants with the assistance of foreign aid, private and government investment and CPEC. However, some of the power plants have been rendered in operational and not connected to the national grid because of lack of supply of fuel or pipeline connectivity, lack of coordination with other energy agencies, etc. In future, adequate planning, technical expertise, economic foresight, coordination must be employed by the government of the day.

CHAPTER 9
Modernizing the Environment

Pakistan's environment encompasses its social and societal milieu, physical settings, civil society, and importantly, state institutions that have largely been left undeveloped and decadent since inception of the country. These facets need to be modernized so as to lift them up in line with the demands of the present century.

Modernization Defined

Many in the country are mistaken and confused about what modernization really is. At the outset Westernization and modernization are two distinct phenomena. Modernization is the wide human condition that arose with the advent of the industrial age, and Westernization is merely one of its aspect. China, Singapore, or Dubai are as modern as any Western nation, yet their culture, language, and traditions are different from one another. Modernization is not about partying all night, alcoholism, drug addiction, loose morals, or unethical behavior. It's about healthy living conditions, safety, and security of life and property. It's about trains running on time and a walk in the park without being molested. It's about tolerance and acceptance of individuals with diverse views and lifestyles. It's about the availability of clean water, emergency medical services, and responsive government agencies.

Collective Efforts

Since modernization impacts all three elements of a nations—individual, society, and state—it requires collective efforts of all three to be effective. To promote democracy and progress in Pakistan, state institutions must be sustained by modern norms and value, and individuals have to adjust with corresponding changes in lifestyle. Society has to formulate rules and evolve with new ethos. The prosperity and well-being of the people does not depend solely on implementation of pure economic steps. An enabling social environment is also needed. The modernization of Pakistan society is critical for two economic reasons—increasing Pakistan's global competitiveness in export markets and achieving high productivity rates domestically.

Generally speaking, Pakistan is a feudal and traditional society with pockets of modernization in big urban cities such as Karachi, Lahore, and Islamabad. With religious beards, hijabs, and prayers everywhere, Pakistan increasingly resembles an indoctrinated, isolated, sullen, cult camp lost in religiosity.[2] This has to change as development and industrialization go hand in hand with modernization. Modernization is the social vehicle for the transformation of the country's traditional, agrarian society to a modern one, and without it, an industrialization Pakistan cannot be transformed from a poor, dysfunctional nation into a modern, progressive one. It's important to remember a country's culture is not static and not etched in stone. It's conducive to change and is always evolving. In this connection the concept of national dress is not fully understood in the country. A national dress is the traditional, historic dress of the people of a country to be worn at special occasions (e.g., kimono of Japan, kilts of Scotland, tracht of Germany, or hanfu of China). These are all national dresses of these countries, but their people don't wear these traditional dresses every day, especially not at work. But Pakistanis have taken their national dress as a dress that must be worn everywhere at all times, even though it might be unsuitable or impractical in the work environment.

Role of Technology

Information and other technology will play a leading role in changing and modernizing the Pakistani society and institutions. Pakistan is on the threshold of digitizing its business and government institutions while the internet and its social media offshoots have already taken a foothold in the urban areas, capturing the imagination of its bulging youth population. The modernization of its society is inevitable and the function of the government should be to act as a catalyst and not as a roadblock. Firewalls and censorship on the internet in the name of culture, morality, or frivolous national interest would be counterproductive and would thwart Pakistan's progress in addition to alienating the youth.

Women's Uplift and Tolerance

Contrary to what many generally believe, most deaths in the world do not occur in wars or on battlefields but in civil society because of gang violence, criminal acts, government brutality, police actions, civilian shootings, etc. [2]More people were killed in Mexico in drug-related violence than the combined death toll of the wars in Iraq and Afghanistan.[2] We must confront this civil violence in Pakistan in a variety of ways, including instilling in citizenry the value of human life and respect for laws and teaching tolerance of others as well as adopting effective law enforcement and policing. Stopping or reducing killings in civic society is linked to the elimination of jihadi terrorism and economic progress.

Maintaining a conducive environment for a modern and progressive society does not simply encompass changes in lifestyle and eating habits. It also means Pakistanis must develop a sense of the law. We cannot harass women on the streets, and we must be aware of our own legal and civil rights. A defining moment of a modern state is the full participation of women in all aspects of its national life.

Various studies have pointed out the unsustainable marginalization of women especially in the workforce, .e.g., *Gender Inequality: A Case Study in Pakistan*, Journal of Scientific Research, Vol 3, No. 3, March 2019. For instance, in banks, corporations, industries, no less than 98% of top mangers are male. There's only a token representation of Pakistani women in sports, media, politics etc. Thousands of young women are brutally murdered in the most heinous form of women subjugation: Honor killings. Sustained, unflinching measures by the government and radical changes in medieval attitudes are a must to eliminate these blemishes and glaring, long-ingrained discrimination against women. Without removing the curse of gender inequality, without the input in productivity from about 50% of the population that women represent, the nation cannot reasonably hope to progress and move forward. Women's uplift and Pakistan's modernization go hand in hand; one cannot be achieved without the other.

Promoting Sports, Health & Culture

It's quite tragic to see the standard of sports in Pakistan drastically taking a nosedive. Once dominant in field hockey and squash, Pakistan is nowhere in the picture now. In track and field, Pakistan performed decently, but now the vision of Abdul Khaliq and Mohammad Iqbal winning gold medals at the Asian Games is a faded memory.

The significance of sports to the nation's well-being cannot be underestimated. It has and will promote national cohesion and bonding in a country driven by ethnic uprisings and socioeconomic disparities. Indeed, sports in Pakistan has proven to be a unifier and force multiplier in fostering Pakistani nationalism.[3] All Pakistanis rooting for our World Cup cricket teams irrespective of being a Balochi, Panjabi, Pashtun, Sindhi, or Mohajir, is a case in point.

A culture of fitness and exercise including all women with a corresponding lifestyle of the citizens would make Pakistan a healthy nation, which in turn would result in increased productivity and decreased medical care costs of the country.[4]

The development and promotion of sports and sporting events not only creates a national Pakistani identity with shared pride, achievement, and togetherness but also fosters the health and fitness of its citizens, which is so crucial for increasing productivity and lessening the national health care costs. In view of the paucity of resources, the country can start with first focusing on sports that do not require expensive facilities, such as soccer or track and field. It can seek inspiration from examples of other not so rich countries such as Kenya, which tops the world in track-and-field events.

In addition to the steps taken toward maintaining the health and fitness of its citizens, the state should provide modern health care facilities to address the basic medical needs of the citizens at a low cost.

If a state is a human body, then culture is its heart. Quite often a mantra is heard in the country that Pakistan is rich in culture. This is true with a caveat. Its culture pertains mostly to its ancient heritage like Gandhari art, Hala pottery,or Khatak dance. Indeed, the nation can be proud of a glorious civilization heritage. But what about the culture of the recent past, the post- independence period? Sadly, the culture of performing arts, music, singing and dancing, have sparingly promoted and developed both by the government and by the civil society. That needs to be changed. It is alarming that after Iqbal, Faiz, Faraz no poets of that caliber are emerging. No upcoming Gulgee or Saqlain in painting either.

A strong focus on cultural development would give a big boost to the nation's psyche. Culture can provide the sorely needed creativity, imagination, entertainment, expression, humanness, tolerance and love to a sullen, moribund, visionless society. Participation of women in performing arts would tend to close the gender gap and would facilitate their unique contribution towards Pakistan's progress. Culture would dramatically uplift the quality of life of its citizens. Finally, religion should not stop cultural advancement. In a country where the sectarian friction and ethnic divide is on a razor's edge the anodyne power of the arts would go a long way in soothing rancor and fostering harmony in diversity.

Honor Killings

Honor killing is a savage, bloodthirsty crime against womenfolk in Pakistan that refuses to go away. Pakistan is generally a male-dominated, patriarchal society, where a man is the final arbiter of the family and upholder of its honor. Thousands of women and young girls of the country have been brutally murdered or stoned to death on the altar of family's honor or *ghairat*. Human Rights Council of Pakistan estimates that more than 1,000 women are thus killed each year in the country. Many honor killings in remote regions goes unreported. Honor killings is a murder of mostly women (very rarely of a male) on the extra marital or pre- marital sex or mere suspicion of it, or for marrying against the family's wishes. This act of murder is carried out by a father, brother, husband or even son, although there have been cases when a mother was also involved in the killing of her daughter.

One of the most shocking incident of honor killing was the murder by the family members in 2011 in the village of *Palas* in remote mountainous Pakistani region of Kohistan of six young girls and boys. Their crime: folk dancing together that was recorded in a video that went viral.

Some concrete steps have been taken by the government to curb this menace. The media's active coverage and exposure of honor killings have helped in reducing its occurrence a little bit. The Pakistan authorities did pass a legislation, the Criminal Law Amendment of 2016, to address, but that do not seem to be making much headway in combating it. Its not the government, or the law enforcement agencies but also the male dominated society in the rural areas and tribal regions that must share the blame. Honor killing is the ultimate in women's subjugation. Pakistani society cannot hope to progress and modernize and show respect and tolerance for the female gender without making these murders a shameful practice of the past. Both the society, the village and tribal leaders especially have to work together with government authorities to combat it.

Whether it's ordained by Islamic religion or not, honor killing has been a part of Muslim history and traditions. The perpetrators of this horrific crime justify it on the grounds of religion and their tribal imperatives, and to protect their family's name and honor. More important, the support of local *mullahs* must be sought to educate the villagers and tribal people of the evilness and non- justification of this act of murder.

CHAPTER 10

Changing State Policy

No foreign policy—no matter how ingenious—has any chance of success if it is born in the minds of a few and carried in the hearts of none.

—Henry Kissinger

Pakistan's Official Position

Pakistan contends that its foreign policy is predicated on some basic principles- the protection of country's territorial integrity and sovereignty as well as the maintenance of peaceful, friendly relations with all countries, especially with Muslim countries of OIC and socioeconomic development of the country. It blames India for the acrimonious relationship between the two countries that erupted immediately after the Partition of the subcontinent in 1947: India's annexation of Jammu and Kashmir in defiance of the United Nations and its refusal to reconcile with the existence of Pakistan as a sovereign state. [1]

Pakistan's core issue remains the settlement of the Kashmir issue as per the 1948 United Nations Security Council (UNSC) resolutions, which called for holding a plebiscite in the Jammu and Kashmir Valley, conditioned on the withdrawal of troops from by both the sides, to settle this pending dispute between the two countries. Pakistan believes that it's on a high moral ground in Kashmir since it is standing up for the freedom and rights of Kashmiris, and the people also believe that in reality India is unlawfully occupying the Kashmir Valley in defiance of the UNSC and international law. India has never reconciled with Pakistan's existence as a sovereign and equal state since it wants Pakistan to submit to its hegemony in the Southeast Asia region. For this purpose, India's actions show that it wants to cripple Pakistan economically and isolate it diplomatically. Pakistan holds that it has been a victim of Indian aggression in four wars, all of which were started by India.[2]

Pakistan does not seek interference in the internal affairs of India or Afghanistan. Though it uses political and diplomatic efforts for the human rights of the Kashmir and Afghani people, it doesn't use proxy terrorism or force to promote these objectives. It desires peaceful relations with India and all its neighbors. On the other hand, Pakistan has been a victim of terrorism, having lost the lives of s60,000 of its citizens.

The Pakistan military denies that its policy toward India is meant to either keep the Kashmir state destabilized by persistent terror attacks sponsored by it or keep the Kashmir issue alive simply for domestic political considerations, thus extracting an inordinate share for the military from the country's budget. Pakistan is merely fighting off India's aggressive designs to impose its hegemony in the region and to bully its smaller neighbor into submission and give up the right of self-determination of the Kashmiri people.

As far as Afghanistan is concerned, Pakistan asserts that it has been an ally and a victim in America's war on terror in Afghanistan. In support of this war, it sacrificed a lot. In fact, approximately 60,000 of its civilians and soldiers were killed by terrorists, and it suffered an economic loss of billions of dollars.

Pakistan's foreign and security policy has always been guided by its desire to safeguard the country's security and territorial integrity and to promote economic progress.[11] Consequently, in the formative years of its independence, Pakistan closely allied itself with the West and United

States during the Cold War through various strategic agreements that provided much needed both military and economic assistance. In 1954 Pakistan signed the Mutual Defense Agreement with USA that soon evolved into larger regional security agreements backed by USA, South East Treaty Organization (SEATO), Regional Cooperation Agreement (RCD) and Central Treaty Organization (CENTO) that included Iran, Turkey besides Pakistan.

After the fall of East Pakistan in 1971, a disappointed Pakistan moved away from the West and trended towards a neutral and Islamic stance. Its focus shifted to the oil rich Arab states in the Middle East for economic support. However, in 1979 with the Soviet invasion of Afghanistan and the subsequent perpetuation of terror insurgency by Taliban and Jihadi forces, Post 9/11 attack, Pakistan was back in the saddle with America and the Coalition as a partner in "War on Terror' declared in 2001. This relationship too soured as Taliban insurgency persisted in Afghanistan and America accused Pakistan of double dealing and not doing enough to fight Taliban, forcing Pakistan to look east towards China for a new alliance.

As proof positive of its policy to seek friendly relations with all countries of the world, Pakistan had recognized the People's Republic of China as early as 1950, becoming the third non- communist country and the first Muslim country to do so. Pakistan became a strategic ally of China in 2015 when it signed the China-Pakistan Economic Corridor (CPEC), a $50 billion project by China to build roads, Gwadar Port, and infrastructure in Pakistan. CPEC is a part of China's ambitious, global and geostrategic Belt and Road Initiative (BRI) mega project which was earlier announced by China to link Asian and African countries via roads, bridges and infrastructure.

Pakistan's official position on its foreign and security policy has been periodically articulated by various government statements, press releases, its spokespersons, its foreign ministers, including Khawaja Asif, Shah Mahmood Qureshi, and Sartaj Aziz, and others in the media such as Munir Akram.[3]

Critical View of Policy

Critics of Pakistan's foreign and security policy hold a different view. Taliban scholar Ahmed Rashid points out two grievous policy errors the country made.[10]

First, at the end of the Cold War, Pakistan decided to "move proxy resources in Kashmir, radicalizing the indigenous Kashmir Movement. Secondly, Gen Musharraf in 2003 decided to resurrect the defeated Afghan Taliban." [12]

It's no secret that for at least three decades Pakistan's military has been waging a low intensity war in India and Afghanistan that involves using its proxy militant or jihadi groups, such as Lashkar-e-Tayyaba (LeT), Jaish-e-Mohammad (JeM), Hizb-ul-Mujahid (HuM0, Haqqani Network (HN), Tehreek-e-Taliban (TTP), Jamat-ud-Dawa (JuW), and other jihadi outfits for carrying out terror attacks in India and Afghanistan. In the opinion of author Apana Paned, Pakistan has adopted this proxy strategy because of two principles or reasons. Firstly, because of Pakistan's s inherent desire to *escape India* and create in Pakistan an anti-India nationalism or identity, and, secondly, because it had limited options in the battlefield. Pakistan military realized that the use of nuclear weapons would be a non-starter for obvious reasons of self-destruction, and in a conventional war Indian forces would overwhelm the smaller Pakistani forces. Hence the military thought that the only way for Pakistan to achieve its goal of parity with India was to use proxy jihadis to fight in India and Kashmir. [12]

Rather than endeavoring for self-reliance and self -development, unfortunately the traditional policy of Pakistani rulers since has always been to seek out major powers of the world for protection, economic aid and diplomatic cover. As former Pakistani ambassador Hussain Haqqani said, "We always had this mythical notion that a rich and powerfully ally will come from outside, solve all our problems." [6]

American administrations from Obama to Trump have been consistently accusing Pakistan of playing a double game, being both an arsonist and a firefighter at the same time. On the one hand, Pakistan took billions of dollars from the United States to help in the fight against the Afghan Taliban, who were ousted by the United States in the post-9//11 war. However, on the other hand, Pakistan did exactly the opposite by helping the Afghan Taliban in their terrorism in Afghanistan against the American-supported Afghan government and by providing the Taliban with safe havens in Pakistan so that they could regroup and plan new terror attacks. [17]

Pakistan vehemently denies this and points to America's own failure to end this long war. In *Directorate S*, which detail the Pakistan-Afghan narrative, security expert Steve Coll blames both the United and Pakistan for the Afghan imbroglio. " Today, we know that hubris and arrogance ... caused America's failure to comprehend the machinations of Pakistan intelligence's secret wing to protect, support and arm the Taliban in terror activities in Afghanistan." [9] However, at present, the United States is engaged in protracted negotiations with the Taliban for peace in Afghanistan with the assistance of Pakistan's army.

The usage of jihadi proxies, such as LeT, JeM, HuM, HN, TTP, TTP, JuD, etc. among others by Pakistan to advance its foreign policy agenda in the region has been widely identified and condemned. Even the Pakistani Prime Minister, Imran Khan, during the recent 2019 session of the United Nation General Assembly, confessed that its army and intelligence service (ISI) supported and trained Al Qaeda and other terror groups. [18]. Previously, in meetings with President Trump, he had conceded the presence of 40,000 jihadi terrorists in his country. Well-known Pakistan expert Professor Christine Fair opines that Pakistan "nurture, support and deploy Islamist proxies to perpetuate a variety of outrages (apparently referring to terror attacks like Pulwama and Mumbai) while using its nuclear weapons umbrella to deter Indian conventional responses and catalyzing American intervention to pressure India to de-escalate." [5] Pakistan, of course, rejects these allegations.

Some critics have dubbed Pakistan as a "warrior state" whose priority is making war and increasing hostilities toward neighbors rather than the development and economic uplift of its own people.[4] South Asian scholar T. V. Paul blames this on Pakistan's "geopolitical curse," which is perhaps similar to the *oil curse* of the Middle East, where its ruler pursues "geopolitically-oriented policies at the expense of political and economic reform." [8]

Adopt New Policy

If the end game of Pakistan is to transform itself into a modern, progressive, prosperous, tolerant, peaceful, and market-oriented nation, it goes without saying that's its foreign policy must be accordingly tailored. And for that objective, the best place to start is resetting relationships with its two neighbors, which have mostly consumed its attention, resources, and efforts.

Four wars, proxy fighting (e.g., the Mumbai, Uri, Pathankot, Indian Parliament, Pulwama), other terror attacks, and the long struggle for Kashmir [14] have sapped Pakistan's political, diplomatic, financial resources, exacerbating the increasing improbability of extracting from India a solution to the Kashmir issue. Pakistan is faced with a security conundrum in the form of the Afghan Taliban and associated terror groups, formerly promoted by it but now out of its control, pursuing their own narrow agendas and fostering political instability in the region. [15] A tipping point has been reached, and it calls for the nation to move forward beyond regional hostilities.[16] If China can put its Taiwan problem on a back burner and move forward, so can we. As far as establishing relations with benefactors China or the Middle East is concerned, Pakistan should avoid the pitfalls of its forces becoming a comprador military and its state a client state: the country must maintain an independent, sovereign policy that keep its national interest paramount.

Having so much in common in terms of history, language, traditions, and/or geography, it's an aberration that Pakistan has so far not been able to establish a mutually beneficial trading relationship with its huge neighbor, India, currently the world's sixth largest economy and rapidly rising. At some point in time—hopefully sooner rather than later—the country must form an economic symbiosis with India that's bound to open doors for its growth. The same goes for Afghanistan. Pakistan has wasted significant resources and lost many lives in vain endeavors to seek strategic depth" by installing a government in Kabul that would dance to our tune.

Peace Bonanza

Assuming that we pursue a peaceful, non -revisionist, noninterfering, and mature policy with all our neighbors, it's bound to bring huge peace dividends to the distraught nation in the form of substantial cuts in defense spending and in the acquisition and development of arms, missiles, and burgeoning nuclear weapons. The door to prosperity would open even wider with open markets and beneficial trade with neighbors. The country can't afford to let India do to it what the United States did to the former USSR. As they say, there's more than one way to skin a cat, and there's more than one way to wage a war. The money thus saved could be spent on developing much-needed infrastructure, paying off national debts, or improving people's welfare. Above all, we will have set a new direction and a new pathway to success.

Elites vs National Interest

Pakistan's persistent problems and challenges that stubbornly refuses to go away have made it somewhat convenient to blame it on the country's elites. It's all the faults of greedy elites and if only they would go away, all the ills that beset the country would also be cured. But its elites are not going to vanish; they are here to stay. As long as there's a state to rule, there would be elites in existence. And as long as there are elites in the state, they would be infighting amongst the elites for power and pelf. Broadly speaking there is a military elite and there is a civilian elite, but in reality there's a military elite composed of army generals and a civilian elite that actually consists of other elites, like feudal elite, *waderas, Maliks, sardars, Khans, Chowdharies,* etc., business and industrial elite, professional elite of doctors, lawyers, academics, bankers, accountants, etc. The struggle amongst all these elites vowing with each other to grab the spoils of power and state resources is neither surprising nor avoidable. It's inevitable. Ideally speaking though, this elitist infighting should only be amongst the civilian elites, and why this is not so in the case of Pakistan is another story. What should be more worrisome for the nation is the question if the elites while infighting are keeping the national interest of the country paramount.

We don't have to refer to Morgenthau or Machiavelli or Beard or Kenneth Arrow or other sophisticated scholars in the field of statecraft to decipher the meaning of Pakistan's national interest. Its national interest is what its people determines it to be, depending on the needs of the time. Staring with the fixed datum of securing the state's physical territory, the basic national interest of Pakistan is its goal or objective of achieving the safety, prosperity and well-being of its people.

Pakistan's national interest is not exclusively locked up in a GHQ vault in Rawalpindi, accessible to a select few. Country's national interest is also providing shoes to a shoeless boy playing soccer in the slum fields of Lyari, medical care to a sick, pregnant woman in the hut dwelling of a village in isolated Balochistan, a paying job to a broken young, unemployed Seraiki man in sizzling Multan.

Any elite vying for power and control of the government of the country must keep this goal supreme over anything else, supreme over its own narrow interests. Unfortunately, Pakistan is witness to seeing its military elite obsessed with perceived external threats to security while losing focus of the goal and objective of the welfare and prosperity of the country's citizens. Civilian elites, whenever they had the opportunity to gain power, have also not fared particularly well in promoting or working for the economic uplift and prosperity of the people. The end result is a country substantially lagging behind other nation states in the region. Even Bangladesh, which was the "sick man" of Pakistan, is now reported to be progressing rapidly, much ahead than the country it separated from in 1971. The progress and prosperity of Pakistan's Asian neighbors is mainly due to their taking the socio-economic goals of their national interests of paramount importance.

Universal Outlook

Much to the detriment of the country's growth and progress, decision makers and implementers of Pakistan's policies have pursued a myopic approach, seeing the world only through the prism of India, Afghanistan, and regional Muslim countries. They have kept the nation isolated from rising Asia and the world beyond though firewalls and censorships, depriving the masses of social, economic, and political connectivity and interaction with the rest of the world. They don't want to acknowledge the importance of allowing access to other people and cultivating the ethos, values, and norms of the evolving universal civilization. The new policy must be based on openness and adopt a universal outlook that will serve as the basis for progress, prosperity, and modernization.

Credit must be given to the country's leaders for a pioneering foreign policy that foresaw close friendly, economic ties China. That policy has borne fruit in the shape of China Pakistan Economic Corrido, a $50 billion economic agreement with Pakistan under which China will provide assistance to build roads, bridges, power and other infrastructure, and develop Port Gwadar in Pakistan, CPEC is basically a part of China's overarching Belt Road Initiative (BRI) geostrategic drive for global interconnectivity through roads and infrastructure But Pakistan's policy toward China should look beyond CPEC. It should attempt to wean Chinese decision makers away from looking at Pakistan through the prism of just another client state and turn them toward the idea of treating Pakistan as a genuine trading, manufacturing, and investment partner.

Overall, as stated earlier, the country's foreign and security policy should be confined to consolidating and monitoring its borders and essentially focusing on developing markets, business, and commerce with all nations. Instead of a closed, paranoid, isolated, security-led approach, an open, confident, commercial, modern, universal outlook is needed in foreign relations. Granted that the country occupies one of the key geostrategic location in the Asian region and should exploit this geographic benevolence to the extent possible and feasible. But any rent seeking should neither be at the cost of country's security interest nor should it override the country's wider national interest of self- reliance. Expert analyst T. V. Paul puts it succinctly, "Pakistan's transformation will only take place if both its strategic circumstances and the ideas and assumptions that the elite hold change fundamentally." Is that a tall order for a policy change? Not really if Pakistan's decision makers get off their high horses and care about its forsaken people with sincerity and rationality.

In matters of executing foreign policy, Pakistan must modernize and fine-tune its diplomatic skills. Some Pakistani embassies abroad are nothing more than glorified madrasas. Its diplomacy lacks the sophistry, finesse, and confidence of the modern times. In the final analysis, both the planning and policy of the state must be guided by the abiding leitmotif, namely the well-being and prosperity of its people.

CHAPTER 11

Food for Thought

(Some of author's previously published Opinions)

1. Is CPEC Enough?
----*December 23, 2017*

The China-Pakistan Economic Corridor (CPEC), however well-intentioned or substantive, may not be enough by itself to transform Pakistan into a viable, modern, and prosperous state. Human societies do not change overnight through concrete edifices alone. Building a modern, dynamic nation is a long, uphill transformation, a process filled with sacrifices.

For instance, take the case of the Marshall Plan. If we go back in history, after the end of the destructive Second World War, America provided huge amounts of economic aid under the Marshall Plan to the vanquished and ruined nations of Germany and Japan in order to rebuild them

However, it was the steely resolve, never-say-die attitude, and relentless hard work of the people of these two nations coupled with the US aid that resulted in their rejuvenation as economic powerhouses. But like the Germans and Japanese back then and like the Chinese and other nations today, are we Pakistanis willing to pay that price and share that burden for a future that embraces security, prosperity, progress, and the welfare of all our citizens?

Unfortunately, we are currently ranked as low as 140 in the socioeconomic index of the nations of the world. To uplift our country from this periphery status to the category of emerging nations, we have to do some heavy lifting. For one, the country has to dramatically increase its production of goods and services (GDP) and must augment its exports to about $50–100 billion annually. To those who say this is impossible to achieve, I beg to differ. With the motivational wind of CPEC at our backs and with some bitter pills to swallow, we can do it.

Our archaic rules and regulations and our inept bureaucracy, which often gives rise to hindrances, corruption, and delays, must be eliminated or streamlined. We need learn and adopt from China such practices as implementation processes, management rules, and effective governance.

Second, it is a huge blunder to allow religious fanaticism and medievalism to run rampant in the country in the name of religious freedom. As we saw in the Faizabad capitulation, this stance shreds to pieces the country's image, political stability, economy, rule of law, and writ of the state. Could such a thing have happened in China? The thousands of madrassas that are basically set up for religious indoctrination should be converted into primary schools. The days and months consumed in religious rituals and frenzy can instead be utilized for productive nation-building activities.

Third, we must reset the country's security and foreign policy from one driven by power and proxy wars to a peaceful, trade-driven, mercantile policy that welcomes all our neighbors and beyond. Such a policy, which has already been adopted by Asian *tiger* states such as Hong Kong and Singapore, would result in huge savings of resources and efforts and also trigger ancillary economic activity, optimizing the CPEC effect.

By applying these guidelines for a modern mind-set, unflinching hard work, and relentless determination with tough, specific measures, the CPEC jumpstart can be the inflection point of our history. It has the potential of moving us closer to becoming a prosperous, modern, peaceful state—a haven for all our citizens and the leitmotif of Pakistan.

2. Pacifying the Beast
—October 22, 2013

We seem to be living in a surreal world. The government goes through the motions of governing. The army goes through the motions of defending. And the people go through the motions of living.

And the Taliban keeps on killing.

Yet deep inside this tragic, surreal milieu, nobody is fooled by the worldly sheen of their uncertain, peripheral existence punctuated by the almost daily thunder of bombs and gunfire jolting them up with periodic doses of reality. We have a bloodthirsty beast in our midst that is becoming increasingly menacing and overpowering with every passing day, casting a long, dark shadow of impending doom that reaches the four corners of our land.

Abject surrender to the Taliban and jihadists not only by the APC politicos but by other segments of the populace makes one hearken back to that sordid chapter of human history when the terrified natives would offer human sacrifices to appease beasts or goddesses of evil.

Here are my questions to those literally begging for peace talks: How many citizens would you be willing to offer to this savage enemy in order to please and pacify them? A hundred? Two hundred? Five hundred citizens a day? I'm sure our leaders can negotiate a reasonable number of our citizens to sacrifice to the Taliban each day to satisfy their blood lust. Then perhaps the beast would leave us alone, and eternal peace would prevail.

Yes, peace must not be at the cost of trashing up of our Constitution, abrogating of our democratic system, death of the Pakistani state as we know it, and beginning of a savage, medieval, totalitarian rule.

And the peace we seek must not result in absolving the murderers and butchers whose hands are stained with the blood and unspeakable suffering and horror of tens of thousands of our men, women and children blown into pieces, beheaded or maimed by these so-called Taliban.

Holding the Taliban and jihadists accountable for the murder and maiming of tens of thousands of innocents is not even an option for the country's gutless, cowardly, Islamist, reactionary, life-hating organizations and people. Where is their vaunted Islamic justice when it comes to the Taliban's atrocities and their crimes?

Forget prosecution and punishment for these heinous crimes. These quivering people would be ecstatic and eternally grateful if the Taliban would only stop their bombings and attacks on our citizens. These brave sons of Islam would choose to grovel in the dust, begging for mercy rather than facing and fighting evil. In his speech at the PMA, the army chief General Kayani said that the army would support and follow the civilian leadership in its policy of confronting the Taliban enemy.

It's funny how the army's newfound respect of civilian leadership never prevented it from dismissing civilian rules before or overthrowing civilian governments or even hanging a civilian prime minister. Many of us believe that the military is hiding behind the skirts of the civilians in order to shirk its primary duty to defend, defeat, and destroy.

Let's examine the nitty-gritty of the prospective peace talks if they are even held. First and foremost, the mere act of Pakistan's representatives sitting on the table with this terror outfit would elevate the Taliban to a state level. Boosted by this surge of sovereignty in their status, the Taliban would thus leave the talks not weakened but further strengthened and emboldened in its ambitions.

Moreover, by agreeing to talks without any conditions, our government will send a very dangerous message that may eventually turn out to be fatal, a message that strikes at the very roots of the country. In a way we would be acknowledging and conceding to the enemy that the state's democratic system, its constitution, its institutions, indeed its very foundation is open for bargaining if enough coercion is applied. Nothing could be more destabilizing to the state's political system.

Talks will set a dangerous precedent for the continuous war against our state. Talks will send the message that brute force, murder, and extortion by terror groups pays and that these are effective tactics against Pakistan. Besides conferring legitimacy on the Taliban, such talks will give them the power and control over our country's future.

But in the heat of the moment, in our exhilarating yearnings for these futile, counterproductive talks that we desperately seek, we must never foolishly delude ourselves into thinking that somehow these doubtful talks would magically end the Taliban's suicide attacks and terrorism.

After all, the Taliban might deem talks to be unnecessary if they come to the conclusion that they are inexorably marching toward achieving their ultimate goal of gaining total control of the Pakistan state without having to go through the rigors of diplomatic niceties. Negotiating skills and political sophistry are not exactly their cup of tea.

Talks or no talks, the whole nation will continue to sink deeper and deeper into a bottomless hole with no way up. Without any will, preparation, and readiness by our nation for an all-out offensive intended to annihilate this diabolical and relentless enemy, the flashes of the few shining novae in our shrinking universe will be rendered dimmer and dimmer.

3. Prerequisites for Pakistan's Survival
—December 28, 2012

First and foremost, we must decisively confront the violence, terrorism, and mayhem being inflicted by the Taliban/jihadists' assault on the state of Pakistan and its people, neutralizing it to an ineffective level if not totally eliminating it. Why? Because these self-confessed enemies of our country have paralyzed the nation's social and economic polity while casting a debilitating net of fear over the country.

This can only be achieved by an all-out, no-holds-barred attack. Half-hearted, piecemeal operations here and there have proven to be catastrophic, playing into Taliban's hands. I know that many people will doubt our ability and capacity to crush terrorism, but if tiny Sri Lanka with its tiny army can do it, then why can't our military with the fifth biggest army in the world finish off this monster once and for all?

Second, in order that justice prevail and solace provided to the victims' families, interlinked with the evanescence of terrorism/jihadism is the need to cleanse the country of the blood of tens of thousands of our murdered innocent citizens through pursuing, prosecuting, and punishing the Taliban/jihadi murderers. Any edifice built on the shaky and guilt-ridden foundation of a blood-soaked soil will not last for long. Only justice for the fallen victims and retribution for the perpetrators can make the country whole again and restore the moral authority and writ of the state. The fact remains that certain people did murder our citizens in cold blood, and they must be held accountable and made to pay for these execrable crimes.

Third, religion-related provisions of our constitution, the fountainhead of our laws, must be discarded or amended. They negate some basic human rights, foster uncertainty and confusion, promote inveterate hatred of other faiths and division among citizens, encourage backwardness, impede progress, and undermine the rule of law.

For instance, on the one hand, the constitution says that all citizens of Pakistan are equal under the law, but on the other hand, it specifies that citizens who are not Muslims cannot become the prime minister or president of the country. Isn't this a most brazen contradiction? Similarly, the constitution also legalizes open discrimination through its Hudood and blasphemy provisions. Moreover, the Constitutional prohibition against laws repugnant to Islamic injunctions and teachings creates utter confusion because these terms are left up in the clouds, undefined, undetermined and open for anybody's interpretation.

The fourth fundamental prerequisite is the abolition of those clauses in our constitution that give unbridled *suo moto* powers to the judiciary—powers unheard of in a democracy. The potential for an ambitious judge abusing this additional and unnecessary jurisdiction can give rise to an unelected part of the government that's answerable to no one, a kind of a state within a state.

Under the pretext of ruling on matters of public importance, national interest, or the enforcement of fundamental rights, a double-talking and usurping judiciary can arbitrarily rule on any matter under the sun. These provisions are a tool by which a conniving and corrupt judiciary can override and arrogate to itself the powers of the other branches of the government, thus subverting the constitution and the sovereign will of the people.

The fifth essential requirement is choosing a set of competent and dynamic leaders to manage our affairs, people who have the strength to lift the nation out of the deep hole of despair, destruction, and doom and who have the fearlessness and vision to steer the ship of the state toward a prosperous, modern, and harmonious harbor.

Many of our citizens may legitimately ask, "What about our burning problems and issues such as good governance, endemic corruption, ubiquitous poverty, massive illiteracy, poor education, suffering health, power and energy shortages, a lack of necessary infrastructure, religious intolerance, fanaticism, safety of life and property, huge unemployment, stunted economic growth, etc.?"

This concern is understandable, but that is precisely the purpose and task of elected leadership and government. They aptly, diligently, and effectively tackle and resolve people's problems and the country's issues within the framework of democracy and freedom. Once the basic, structural requirements are met, the elected government and the nation will be poised and ready to handle and effectively resolve national issues and its people's problems.

The nation's quest for realizing its destiny lies in tatters. Our march for progress and prosperity has been brought to a grinding halt as a result of the pernicious effects of the factors highlighted in this book. Are we strong and determined enough to take the bull by the horn and challenge these destructive forces? Or are we weak and content to kick the can further down the road?

If we opt to choose the latter course and leave the next or future generations to confront and remedy these fundamental defects, then we run the risk of accepting—and perhaps condoning—the fact that there might not be a next generation of Pakistani citizens.

CHAPTER 12

Conclusion

*The future is not something we arrive at so much as something
we create through our actions in the present.*

—Douglas Rushkoff

If anything, Pakistan's turbulent seventy years of history has shown its resiliency and collective determination to continue to exist as a nation-state. It's not going anywhere. It's here to stay. But the million-dollar question is this: What kind of a state will it stay as?

The Pakistani Dream

It cannot stay as an increasingly radicalized theocratic state. That would doom it to medievalism and irrelevance in the twenty-first century, unconnected to the present-day exigencies. It cannot be a revisionist garrison state, moribund and isolated, wasting it energy and resources on hostilities with other nations. In order to be a viable and successful state, it must aim and endeavor to be a modern, market-oriented, tolerant Muslim welfare state pursuing the Pakistani dream of well-being, prosperity, security, and fulfillment for all its downtrodden people.

That journey starts with first providing education to its millions of young children. It starts with discarding old assumptions and obsolete ideas. It starts with the state and society taking determined steps toward evanescence of jihadi terrorism and medieval mind-sets and the emergence of a modern, robust, ethical polity. It starts with adopting constitutional measures, fostering an effective democracy and norms with social and economic freedom, revamping various national institutions, strategizing about economic development, eliminating terrorism and the extremist mind-sets, modernizing the milieu. And changing state policy along the lines suggested in this book.

Rulers in power must remember that political stability and economic certainty in Pakistan provide the bedrock for the economic recovery and prosperity of the nation. And divisive politics and political vendettas will destroy this foundation and turn such long-cherished hope into a wistful illusion. The advent of a new, courageous, and wise leadership is essential to achieving these noble aims.

Finally, it's ironical that in this interdependent world, each state is left to its own devices for survival and independence. This is what it is—a battle of survival by each state. To survive as a viable state, to improve the deprived standard of living, Pakistan and its people must innovate, reinvent, reform, refocus, or do whatever it takes to achieve that end. All its policy must be single-mindedly geared toward attaining that goal.

Unfortunately, Pakistan has had a history of seeking out and depending upon the deep pocket of other world powers to take care of its economic problems, to prop it up, and to provide it with arms and money. In the halcyon days of the Cold War, it relied on the West and the United States for material and diplomatic support. During the years after 9/11, it depended again on the United States for billions to wage the war on terror and then on the dole of oil-rich Sunni Arabs to do their bidding against the threat of Ayatollah's regime. Now it depends on the construction of the Chinese CPEC and financing in return for playing the role of China's strategic satellite in the Asian theater. Pakistan must understand that it is this policy of reliance on external sugar daddies to the exclusion of its own serious, domestic efforts to grow its economy and plan for the future that has brought the nation to its knees. And if it continues with the same set of disastrous policies, it should expect the same outcome.

The better future we desire as a Pakistani nation will not arrive because of good intentions, noble goals, and fervent prayers. It has to be shaped by actions and decisions that the state as well as the people of Pakistan take. The litany of actions in all fields and institutions humbly suggested in this work are by no means exclusive, final, or complete. These proposals are basically meant to serve as trigger points for the transformation of the state and society. Hopefully, the arc of history— in the case of Pakistan—bends in the right direction.

If the state and people of Pakistan do not begin to change in the ways alluded to here, its Asian neighbors will smoothly sail by in this century and beyond, while Pakistan, stuck in the past, will recede further and further and become an isolated island. As connectivity and togetherness of people across the globe increases exponentially, thanks to the miracle of IT, rigid ideology becomes less appealing to the world. . Pakistan's obsessive religious self-identification, which has an inherent tendency to excoriate international assimilation. can be deleterious to its progress and prosperity. Finally, the people must always bear in mind the reversibility of the country's fragile democracy, which will require constant attention. The future of Pakistan rests with the real decisions and actions that the state and the individuals take. The country must smell the roses of the possible, achievable future rather than clasping the dried leaves of the surly past.

Epilogue

Pakistan's prime minster Imran Khan and his political party, Pakistan Tehreek- e -Istiqlal (PTI) has just completed one year in office, and the news from Islamabad is not good. Coming into power in 2018 through disputed elections, celebrity Khan has been lurching from crisis to crisis ever since.

Numbers don't lie and all the leading economic indicators seems to point towards to a near bankrupt economy, buoyed by a lifeline thrown by International Monetary Fund (IMF) in the form of a $6 billion bailout package. Double-digit inflation and interest rate, massive unemployment of teeming youth, largest fiscal deficit in history, amounting to an unprecedented Rs 3.4 trillion or 8.9% of country's GDP, largest increase in debts and liabilities in a single year totaling Rs 40 trillion including $120 billion in foreign debts, shrinkage of national economy from $348 billion to $280 billion, and 40% devaluation of local currency paints an unsustainable economic scenario. Investment has almost dried up as business activities have alarmingly slowed down. Both are result of Government's incessant U-turns in policy and witch hunt on the pretext of corruption fighting. Much needed revenue collection has dipped instead of rising. Critics blame the regime's fiscal mismanagement and sheer incompetence for the fiasco.

On the domestic front, it's not a rosy picture either. To eliminate criticism and challenge, the government has effectively muzzled the media, silenced dissent and jailed the leading political opponents. A wide array of repressive tactics was employed against the newspapers and TV channels, ranging from coercion, physical assault, jail, threats, dismissal, midnight knocks, censorship. Prominent political leaders, including former prime ministers and president were imprisoned, tortured and persecuted.

Unsuccessful attempts were made to crush ethnic uprisings in KPK and Balochistan provinces. Though on the surface a semblance of political stability seems to prevail, a gnawing sense of chaos and uncertainty lurks on the national horizon.

In foreign affairs, the Imran Khan Government suffered a devastating setback when India shockingly checkmated it by revoking Article 370 of the Indian Constitution that had kept alive the "disputed status ' of Jammu & Kashmir region. This Indian action caught the Khan regime completely unaware and unprepared. In one stroke, Indian Government nullified 70 years of Pakistan's painstaking, costly efforts on wresting Kashmir from India.

Economic and political challenges aside, Khan's big test remains. Can he successfully persuade the military establishment to change the direction of the state's foreign and security policy from one of civilian control and hostilities to one of non-interference and peaceful relations.

References

Foreword

1   Yasmin Khan, *The Great Partition: The Making of India and Pakistan* (New Haven, CT: Yale University Press, 2007).
2   Maulana Abul Kalam Azad, *India Wins Freedom* (Stosius Inc./Advent Book Division, 1978).
3   Hector Bolitho, *Jinnah: Creator of Pakistan* (London: Oxford University Press—Pakistan, 2006).
4   Larry Collins and Dominique Lapierre, *Freedom at Midnight* (Ram Nagar, New Delhi: Vikas Publishing House, 2001).
5   Stephen Cohen, *The Idea of Pakistan* (Washington, DC: Brooking Institution Press, 2004).

Chapter 1: Crisis Galore

1   Ayesha Jalal, *The Struggle for Pakistan* (Cambridge, MA: Harvard University Press 2019).
2   Population by countries (2019) https://www.worldometers.info.world-population.
3   Nabeel Qader, "Pakistan Water Crisis," *Express Tribune*, February 16t, 2019.
4   Sumit Ganguly and S. Paul Kapur, *India, Pakistan, and the Bomb* (New York: Columbia University Press, 2010).
5   Federation of American Scientists, "Pakistan Nuclear Weapons: A Brief History," https://www.fax.org/nuke/guide/Pakistan/nuke.

Chapter 2: Moving Forward

1   M. D. Staff, "People Can Prosper and Thrive If Pakistan Reforms Faster," https://www.moderndiplomacy.com, March, 19, 2019.

2   Humera Iqtedar and David Gilmartin, "Secularism and the State in Pakistan," *Modern Asian Studies* 45, no. 3 (May 2011).

3   Lawrence Freedman, *Strategy: A History* (New York: Oxford University Press, 2013).

4   Douglas Rushkoff, *Team Human* (New York: H. W. Norton & Co., 2019).

5   Daron Acemoglu and James A. Robinson, *Why Nations Fail: The Origins of Power, Prosperity, and Poverty* (New York: Crown Business, 2012).

6   Joseph A. Tainter, *The Collapse of Complex Societies* (New York: Cambridge University Press, 1988).

7   Steven Levitsky and Daniel Zibleth, *How Democracies Die* (New York: Crown Publishing Group, 2018).

8   Naseer Dashti. *The Baloch and Pakistan* (London: Trafford Publishing Inc, 2012).

9   Aurangzeb Alamgir, *Pakistan's Baloch Problem, World Affairs*, Vol175, No 4, (Thousand Island, CA: Sage Publications, Inc., 2013).

10 Abbas Notezar, *Balochistan Short History* (Lahore: The Monthly View Point, 2015).

11 Charles Krauthammer, *Things That Matter: Three Decades of Passions, Pastimes and Politics*: New York: Penguin Random House, 2013).

Chapter 3: Introspection: Assault on the Constitution

1   Hamid Khan, *Constitutional History of Pakistan* (London, UK: Oxford University Press, 2005).

2   Mohammad Hanif, "Pakistan's Judges Are on a Mission. But What Is It?" *New York Times*, March 1, 2018.

3   Third Schedule, Articles 178 and 194, Pakistan Constitution.

4   Liaqat Ali Khan, "Just One More Coup Will Undo Pakistan," *Huffington Post*, October 15, 2007.

5   *Maulvi Tamizuddin Khan case*, PLD 1955 SC 240.

6   Inam R. Sehri, *Judges and Generals in Pakistan* (Surrey, UK: Grosvenor House Publishing, 2012).

7   Mohammad Idris and Naushad Khan, "A Survey of Role of Judiciary in Validating Military and Authoritarian Regimes in Pakistan," *Open Access Journal*, https://www.omicsonline.org, 2018.

8   A. J. Baloch and G. M. Gaho, "Military Interventions in Pakistan and Its Implications," *The Government-Annual Research Journal of Political Science.*

9   Ayesha Siddiqa, *Military Inc.* (London: Oxford University Press, 2007).

10 Aqil Shah, *The Army and Democracy* (Cambridge, MA: Harvard University Press, 2014)

11 Naghman Khan, "Pakistan's First Military Coup," Naval Postgraduate School, 2012.

12 Yaser Hamdani, "Role of Judiciary in Pakistan," *India Today*, August 10, 2012.

13 Ian Talbot, *Pakistan: A Modern History* (New York: St. Martin's Press, 1998).

14 Satish Kumar, "Judicial Subservience Hampered Democracy in Pakistan," *South Asia Perspective*, 2007.

15 Zulfiqar Ali Bhutto, *If I Am Assassinated* (New Delhi: Vikas Publishing House, 1979).

16 Brian Coughley, *A History of the Pakistan Army* (New York: Carrel Books, 2016).

17 "Pakistan's Top Court is eager to take on any brief," *The Economist*, March 28, 2018.

18 *Imran Khan Niazi v. Mian Mohammad Nawaz Sharif*, 2017 SC 265 .

19 Hameed Haroun, "A Dirty War on Freedom of Press in Pakistan," *Washington Post*, July 11, 2018.

20 Hannan R. Hussain, "Press Freedom under Siege in Pakistan," *The Diplomat*, December 12, 2018, http://www.thediplomat.com.

21 Cyril Almeida, "Battering down Award-winning journalist," *Al Jazeera*, April 24, 2019,

22 Hasnat Malik, "Videogate: Judge Arshad Malik requests 'foolproof' security," *The News*, July 15, 2019, https://www.thenews.com.pk.

Chapter 4: Correcting the Constitution

1   The Constitution of Pakistan, https://www.pakistani.org/constitution/.

2   Tamzil-ur-Rehman, *Objectives Resolution and Its Impact on Pakistan Constitution and Law* (Karachi City, Sindh: Royal Book Co., 1996).

3   Nasim Hasan Shah, "Judgements on the Constitution, Rule of Law, And Martial Law," *Wajidalis*, 1986.

4   Asad Jamal and Maryam Khan, "Does Pakistan need to revisit its Constitution," August 13, 2006, https://www.dawn.com

5   Richard A. Fallon, Jr., "Legitimacy and Constitution," *Harvard Law Review* 118 (April 2006): 5,161.

6   Andre Mermor, *"Are Constitutions Legitimate?" Cornell University Law School, Faculty Publications* (2007).

7   .Alaa M. Bokhari, "The Constitution of Pakistan Issues: Challenges and Options," https:///www.academia.edu/556065/.

8   Dr. Syed Jaffer Ahmed, *Overview of the Constitution of Pakistan* (Lahore: Pakistan of Legislative Development, 2004).

Chapter 5: Pakistani Welfare Nationalism

1   Dr. Monis Ahmer, "Myth of Pakistan Nationalism," August 14, 2014, https://www.dawn.com.

2   Yoram Hazony, *The Virtue of Nationalism* (New York: Basic Books, 2018).

3   Objectives Resolution, https://www.historypath.com.

4   Sharif Al Mujahid, "Sir Syed Ahmed Khan and Pakistan Nationalism in India," *Islamic Research Institute, Islamic Studies*, no. 1 (1988).

5   Sophie Duur, "Partitioning India: Indian Muslim Nationalism and the Origins of the Muslim State (1800–1947)," https://www.scholar.colorado.edu.

6   K. K. Aziz, *British and Muslim India* (London: Heinemann, 1963).

7   Saad Khairi, *Jinnah Reinterpreted: The Journey from Indian Nationalism to Pakistan Statehood* (London: Oxford University Press, 1995).

8   Sohaib Mukhtar, *Social Transformation of Pakistan under the Objectives Resolution* (Malaysia: National University of Malaysia, 2017).

9   Andreas Wimmer, "Why Nationalism Works," *Foreign Affairs*, March/April 2019, https://www.foreignaffairs.com/articles/.

10 Lois-Eric Cederman, "Blood for Soil," *Foreign Affairs*, March/April 2019, https://www.foreignaffairs.com/articles .

Chapter 6: Reforming the Institutions

1   www.na.gov.pk/.

2   www.senate.gov.pk.

3   https://en.wikipedia.org/wiki/NationalAssembly_of_Pakistan.

4   https://en.wikipedia.org/wiki/Senate_of_Pakistan.

5   https://www.cabinet.gov.pk.

6   Ishrat Hussain, *Governing the Ungovernable: Institutional Reforms for Democratic Governance* (London: Oxford University Press, 2018).

7   Khadim Hussain, "Building a new order," March 14, 2019, https://www.dawn.com.

8   National Commission on Government Reforms Report (2008)

9   Andrew Wilder, "The Politics of Civil Service Reforms in Pakistan," *Journal of International Affairs* 63, no.1 (Fall/Winter 2009).

10   Dr Faqir Hussain, "The Judicial System of Pakistan," 2007, https://www.Ijcp.gov.pk.

11   International Crisis Group, Asia Report No. 160, "Reforming the Judiciary in Pakistan," 2008, https://iconow.org/document/160_reforming_the_judiciary_in_Pakistan.

12   Osama Siddique, *Approaches to Legal and Judicial Reforms in Pakistan* (Cambridge: Cambridge University Press, 2013).

13   Tariq Khosa, "Reforms for progress," *Daily Dawn*, December 10, 2018, https://www.dawn.com.

14   Nadia Naviwala, "Pakistan Education Crisis: The Real Story," 2019, https://www.wilsoncenter.org.

15   Wajid Ali Syed, "Pakistan loses appeal against Broadsheet, to pay Rs 5.21 billion penalty," *The Daily News*, July 13, 2019, https://www.thenews.com.pk.

16   Fabrice Arfi and Lhome, "Le Contract, Karachi," https://www.Mediaport.com

17   Nasim Zehra, *From Kargil to the Coup: Events that Shook Pakistan* (London: Oxford University Press, 2018).

18   Inam R. Sehri, *Judges and Generals in Pakistan* (Surrey, UK: Governor House Publishing, 2012).

Chapter 7: Fighting Terrorism and Extremism

1   Pamela Constable, *Playing with Fire: Pakistan at War with Itself* (New York: Random House, 2011).

2   Steve Coll, *Ghost Wars* (London: Penguin Books, 2004).

3   Benjamin R. Barber, *Jihad vs Macworld* (New York: Random House, 1995).

4   United Nations, "Global Counter-terrorism Strategy, Approved Sept 8, 2006," https://www.un.org/counterterrorism/.

5   Crisis Group, "Revisiting Counter-terrorism Strategies in Pakistan: Opportunities and Pitfalls," Report no. 271, Asia, 2015, https://www.crisisgroup.com.

6   Dhruva Jainshankar, "Pakistan Has No More Excuses for Supporting Terrorism," *Foreign Policy*, February 15, 2019.

7   Bill Roggio, "Pakistan charges 13 Lashkar e Taiba leaders under Anti-Terrorism Act," *FDD's Long War Journal*, July 13, 2019. .

Chapter 8: Strategizing the Economy

1   Susan L. Shirk, *China: Fragile Superpower* (New York: Oxford University Press, 2007).
2   Steven Pinker, *Enlightenment Now* (New York: Penguin 2014).
3   Akbar Zaidi, *Issues in Pakistan's Economy* (New York: Oxford University Press, 2015).
4   Fasih Uddin, *Pakistan Economic Journey: Need for a New Paradigm* (Rome: IPS Press, 2019).
5   Shahid Javed Burki, Iftikhar Ahmed, and Ejaz Choudhary, *Pakistan at Seventy* (Rutledge, 2019).
6   Yi Wen, "China's Rapid Rise from Backward Agrarian Society to Industrial Powerhouse, April 12, 2016, https://www.stlouisfed.org.
7   Kaiser Bengali, "Pakistan's casino economy," *Daily Dawn*, September 20, 2015, https://www.dawn.com.
8   Ishrat Hussain, *Governing the Ungovernable* (New York: Oxford University Press, 2018).
9   Sakib Sharami, "A challenging context," *Daily Dawn*, July 5, 2019, https://www.dawn.com.
10 Yi Wen, "China's Rapid Rise from Backward Agrarian Society to Industrial Powerhouse in Just 35 Years," April 12, 2016, https://www.stlouisfed.org.
11 Khaleeq Kinai, "Pakistan to pay dearly for 'expropriating' assets of Turkish firm Karkey," *Daily Dawn*, September 22, 2017.

Chapter 9: Modernizing the Environment

1   Rachel Kleinfield, *A Savage Order* (New York: Penguin Books, 2018).
2   Anatol Lieven, *Pakistan: A Hard Country* (Perseus Book Group, 2012).
3   Oraulf Seippel, "Sports and Nationalism in a Globalized World," *International Journal of Sociology* 47 (2019).
4   Connor, "Impact of Sport on Human Society," October 20, 2014, https://www.artsite.tv/.
5   Lawrence Harrison and Samuel P. Huntington, *Culture Matters* (New York: Basic Books, 2000).

Chapter 10: Changing State Policy

1   Pakistan's Public Diplomacy, Ministry of Foreign Affairs, Government of Pakistan, http://www.mofa.gov.pk.

2   Munir Akram, "Foreign Policy Agenda," *Daily Dawn*, December 21, 2018, https://www.dawn.com.

3   Munir Akram, "Opportunities and Challenges in Pakistan Foreign Policy," *Global Village Space*, August 18, 2018.

4   T. N. Paul, *The Warrior State* (New York: Oxford University Press, 2014).

5   Christine C. Fair, *Pakistan Army: Fighting to the End* (New York: Oxford University Press, 2014).

6   Hussain Haqqani, *Reimagining Pakistan* (India: HarperCollins Publishers, 2018).

7   Ayesha Siddiqa, *Military Inc: Inside Pakistan's Military Economy* (New York: Penguin, 2007).

8   T. N. Paul, *The Warrior State* (New York: Oxford University Press, 2014).

9   Steve Coll, *Directorates S* (New York: Penguin, 2019).

10 Michael Lewis, *The Fifth Risk* (New York: W. W. Norton & Co., 2018).

11 Sartaj Aziz, Council on Foreign Affairs Interview, March 1, 2016.

12 Ahmed Rashid, *Pakistan on the Brink* (New York: Penguin, 2012).

13 Apana Pnade, *Explaining Pakistan's Foreign Policy: Escaping India* (New York: Routeledge, 2001).

14 Alaster Lamb, *Kashmir: A Disputed Legacy, 1884–1990* (Hertford, Hertfordshire: Roxford Books, 1991).

15 Mathew P. Taylor, "Pakistan's Kashmir Policy and Strategy since 1947," thesis, Naval Postgraduate School, Monterey, CA, 2004.

16 Tariq Ali, *Kashmir: The Case for Freedom* (London: Verso Books, 2011).

17 Farzana Sheikh, *Making Sense of Pakistan* (New York: Oxford University Press, 2018).

18 Aqil Shah, *The Army and Democracy: Military Politics* (Cambridge, MA: Harvard Press, 2014).

Index

C

D

E

F

G

H

I

بسم الله الرحمن الرحيم

(In the name of Allah, the most Beneficent,
the most Merciful.)

THE CONSTITUTION OF THE ISLAMIC
REPUBLIC OF PAKISTAN

[12TH APRIL, 1973]

Preamble

Whereas sovereignty over the entire Universe belongs to Almighty Allah alone, and the authority to be exercised by the people of Pakistan within the limits prescribed by Him is a sacred trust;

And whereas it is the will of the people of Pakistan to establish an order;

Wherein the State shall exercise its powers and authority through the chosen representatives of the people;

Wherein the principles of democracy, freedom, equality, tolerance and social justice, as enunciated by Islam, shall be fully observed;

Wherein the Muslims shall be enabled to order their lives in the individual and collective spheres in accordance with the teachings and requirements of Islam as set out in the Holy Quran and Sunnah;

Wherein adequate provision shall be made for the minorities freely to profess and practise their religions and develop their cultures;

Wherein the territories now included in or in accession with Pakistan and such other territories as may hereafter be included in or accede to Pakistan shall form a Federation wherein the units will be autonomous with such boundaries and limitations on their powers and authority as may be prescribed;

Wherein shall be guaranteed fundamental rights, including equality of status, of opportunity and before law, social, economic and political justice, and freedom of thought, expression, belief, faith, worship and association, subject to law and public morality;

Wherein adequate provision shall be made to safeguard the legitimate interests of minorities and backward and depressed classes;

Wherein the independence of the judiciary shall be fully secured;

161

Wherein the integrity of the territories of the Federation, its independence and all its rights, including its sovereign rights on land, sea and air, shall be safeguarded;

So that the people of Pakistan may prosper and attain their rightful and honoured place amongst the nations of the World and make their full contribution towards international peace and progress and happiness of humanity;

Now, therefore, we, the people of Pakistan;

Conscious of our responsibility before Almighty Allah and men;

Cognisant of the sacrifices made by the people in the cause of Pakistan;

Faithful to the declaration made by the Founder of Pakistan, Quaid-i-Azam Mohammad Ali Jinnah, that Pakistan would be a democratic State based on Islamic principles of social justice;

Dedicated to the preservation of democracy achieved by the unremitting struggle of the people against oppression and tyranny;

Inspired by the resolve to protect our national and political unity and solidarity by creating an egalitarian society through a new order;

Do hereby, through our representatives in the National Assembly, adopt, enact and give to ourselves, this Constitution.

PART I

Introductory

The Republic and its territories

[1]**1.**   (1)   Pakistan shall be Federal Republic to be known as the Islamic Republic of Pakistan, hereinafter referred to as Pakistan.

[2][(2)   The territories of Pakistan shall comprise—

(a)   the Provinces of [3][Balochistan], the [4][Khyber Pakhtunkhwa], the Punjab and [5][Sindh];

(b)   the Islamabad Capital Territory, hereinafter referred to as the Federal Capital;

(c)   the Federally Administered Tribal Areas; and

(d)   such States and territories as are or may be included in Pakistan, whether by accession or otherwise.

(3)   [6][Majlis-e-Shoora (Parliament)] may by law admit into the Federation new States or areas on such terms and conditions as it thinks fit.]

Islam to be State religion

2.   Islam shall be the State religion of Pakistan.

The Objectives Resolution to form part of substantive provisions

[7][**2A.** The principles and provisions set out in the Objectives Resolution reproduced in the Annex are hereby made substantive part of the Constitution and shall have effect accordingly].

---

[1]   The provisions of the Constitution except those of Articles 6, 8 to 28, (both inclusive), clauses 2 and (2a) of Article 101, Articles 199, 213 to 216 (both inclusive) and 270-A, brought into force with effect from 10th March, 1985, *ride* S.R.O. No. 212(I)/85. dated 10th March, 1985, Gazette of Pakistan, Extraordinary, Part-II, page 279 and the aforesaid Articles brought into force with effect from 30th December, 1985, *vide* S.R.O. No. 1273(I)/85 dated 29th December. 1985, Gazette of Pakistan, Extraordinary, Part-II, page 3185.
[2]   Subs. by the Constitution (First Amdt.) Act, 1974 (33 of 1974), s. 2, for "clauses (2), (3) and (4)" (w.e.f; the 4th May, 1974).
[3]   Subs. By the Constitution (Eighteenth Amdt.) Act, 2010 (10 of 2010), s. 3 for –Baluchistan."
[4]   Subs. *ibid.,* for –North-West-Frontier".
[5]   Subs. *ibid.,* for –Sind".
[6]   Subs. by the Revival of the Constitution of 1973 Order, 1985 (P.O. No. 14 of 1985), Art. 2 and Sch., for "Parliament".
[7]   New Article 2A Ins. *Ibid.*

Elimination of exploitation

3. The State shall ensure the elimination of all forms of exploitation and the gradual fulfillment of the fundamental principle, from each according to his ability to each according to his work.

Right of individuals to be dealt with in accordance with law, etc.

4. (1) To enjoy the protection of law and to be treated in accordance with law is the inalienable right of every citizen. Wherever he may be, and of every other person for the time being within Pakistan.

    (2)   In particular—

        (a) no action detrimental to the life, liberty, body, reputation or property of any person shall be taken except in accordance with law;

        (b) no person shall be prevented from or be hindered in doing that which is not prohibited by law; and

        (c) no person shall be compelled to do that which the law does not required him to do.

Loyalty to State and obedience to Constitution and law

5. (1)   Loyalty to the State is the basic duty of every citizen.

    (2)   Obedience to the Constitution and law is the [1][inviolable] obligation of every citizen wherever he may be and of every other person for the time being within Pakistan.

High treason

6. [2][(1)   Any person who abrogates or subverts or suspends or holds in abeyance, or attempts or conspires to abrogate or subvert or suspend or hold in abeyance, the Constitution by use of force or show of force or by any other unconstitutional means shall be guilty of high treason.]

    (2)   Any person aiding or abetting [3][or collaborating] the acts mentioned in clause (1) shall likewise be guilty of high treason.

---

[1] Subs. by P. O. No. 14 of 1985, Art. 2 and Sch., for "basic".
[2] Subs. by the Constitution (Eighteenth Amdt.) Act. 2010 (10 of 2010), s.4 for –clause (1)".
[3] Ins. *Ibid.*

^{1}[(2A) An act of high treason mentioned in clause (1) or clause (2) shall not be validated by any court including the Supreme Court and a High Court.]

(3) ^{2}[Majlis-e-Shoora (Parliament)] shall by law provide for the punishment of persons found guilty of high treason.

———

PART II

Fundamental Rights and Principles of Policy

Definition of the State

7.   In this Part, unless the context otherwise requires, "the State" means the Federal Government, [1][Majlis-e-Shoora (Parliament)], a Provincial Government, a Provincial Assembly, and such local or other authorities in Pakistan as are by law empowered to impose any tax or cess.

CHAPTER 1. – FUNDAMENTAL RIGHTS

Laws inconsistent with or in derogation of Fundamental Rights to be void

8.   (1)   Any law, or any custom or usage having the force of law, in so far as it is inconsistent with the rights conferred by this Chapter, shall, to the extent of such inconsistency, be void.

(2)   The State shall not make any law which takes away or abridges the rights so conferred and any law made in contravention of this clause shall, to the extent of such contravention, be void.

(3)   The Provisions of this Article shall not apply to—

(a) any law relating to members of the Armed Forces, or of the police or of such other forces as are charged with the maintenance of public order, for the purpose of ensuring the proper discharge of their duties or the maintenance of discipline among them; or

[2][(b) any of the —

(i) laws specified in the First Schedule as in force immediately before the commencing day or as amended by any of the laws specified in that Schedule;

---

[1]   *See* footnote 6 on page 3, *supra*

[2]   Subs. by the Constitution (Fourth Amdt.) Act, 1975 (71 of 1975), s. 2, for "paragraph (b)", *(w.e.f* the 21st November, 1985), which was previously amended by Act 33 of 1974, s. 3, *(w.e.f* 4th May, 1974).

(ii) other laws specified in Part I of the First Schedule;]

and no such law nor any provision thereof shall be void on the ground that such law or provision is inconsistent with, or repugnant to, any provision of this Chapter.

(4)   Notwithstanding anything contained in paragraph (b) of clause (3), within a period of two years from the commencing day, the appropriate Legislature shall bring the laws specified in [1][Part II of the First Schedule] into conformity with the rights conferred by this Chapter :

Provided that the appropriate Legislature may by resolution extend the said period *of* two years by a period not exceeding six months.

Explanation.– If in respect of any law [2][Majlis-e-Shoora (Parliament)] is the appropriate Legislature, such resolution shall be a resolution of the National Assembly.

(5)   The rights conferred by this Chapter shall not be suspended except as expressly provided by the Constitution.

Security of person

9.   No person shall be deprived of life or liberty save in accordance with law.

Safeguards as to arrest and detention

10.   (1)   No person who is arrested shall be detained in custody without being informed, as soon as may be, of the grounds for such arrest, nor shall he be denied the right to consult and be defended by a legal practitioner of his choice.

(2)   Every person who is arrested and detained in custody shall be produced before a magistrate within a period of twenty-four hours *of* such arrest, excluding the time necessary for the journey from the place of arrest to the court of the nearest magistrate, and no such person shall be detained in custody beyond the said period with out the authority of a magistrate.

(3)   Nothing in clauses (1) and (2) shall apply to any person who is arrested or detained under any law providing for preventive detention.

---

[1] Subs. by the Constitution (Fourth Amdt.) Act, 1975 (71 of 1975), s. 2, for "the First Schedule, not being a law which relates to, or is connected with, economic reforms."

[2] *See* footnote 6 on page 3, *supra*

(4) No law providing for preventive detention shall be made except to deal with persons acting in a manner prejudicial to the integrity, security or defence of Pakistan or any part thereof, or external affairs of Pakistan, or public order, or the maintenance of supplies or services, and no such law shall authorise the detention of a person for a period exceeding [1][three months] unless the appropriate Review Board has, after affording him an opportunity of being heard in person, reviewed his case and reported, before the expiration of the said period, that there is, in its opinion, sufficient cause for such detention, and, if the detention is continued after the said period of '[three months], unless the appropriate Review Board has reviewed his case and reported, before the expiration of each period of three months, that there is, in its opinion, sufficient cause for such detention.

Explanation I.— In this Article, "the appropriate Review Board" means,

(i) in the case of a person detained under a Federal law, a Board appointed by the Chief Justice of Pakistan and consisting of a Chairman and two other persons, each of whom is or has been a Judge of the Supreme Court or a High Court; and

(ii) in the case of a person detained under a Provincial law, a Board appointed by the Chief Justice of the High Court concerned and consisting of a Chairman and two other persons, each of whom is or has been a Judge of a High Court.

Explanation II.—The opinion of a Review Board shall be expressed in terms of the views of the majority of its members.

(5)   When any person is detained in pursuance of an order made under any law providing for preventive detention, the authority making the order shall, [2][within fifteen days] from such detention, communicate to such person the grounds on which the order has been made, and shall afford him the earliest opportunity of making a representation against the order :

Provided that the authority making any such order may refuse to disclose facts which such authority considers it to be against the public interest to disclose.

(6)   The authority making the order shall furnish to the appropriate Review Board all documents relevant to the case unless a

---

[1] Subs. by the Constitution (Third Amdt.) Act, 1975 (22 of 1975), s. 2, for "one month" (*w.e.f.* the 13th February. 1975).

[2] Subs. *ibid.*, for "as soon as may be, but not later than one week" (*w.e.f.* the 13th February, 1975).

certificate, signed by a Secretary to the Government concerned, to the effect that it is not in the public interest to furnish any documents, is produced.

(7)   Within a period of twenty-four months commencing on the day of his first detention in pursuance of an order made under a law providing for preventive detention, no person shall be detained in pursuance of any such order for more than a total period of eight months in the case of a person detained for acting in a manner prejudicial to public order and twelve months in any other case :

Provided that this clause shall not apply to any person who is employed by, or works for, or acts on instructions received from, the enemy [1][, or who is acting or attempting to act in a manner prejudicial to the integrity, security or defence of Pakistan or any part thereof or who commits or attempts to commit any act which amounts to an anti-national activity as defined in a Federal law or is a member of any association which has for its objects, or which indulges in, any such anti national activity].

(8)   The appropriate Review Board shall determine the place of detention of the person detained and fix a reasonable subsistence allowance for his family.

(9)   Nothing in this Article shall apply to any person who for the time being is an enemy alien.

Right to fair trial

[2][10A. For the determination of his civil rights and obligations or in any criminal charge against him a person shall be entitled to a fair trial and due process.]

Slavery, forced labour, etc., prohibited

11.   (1)   Slavery is non-existent and forbidden and no law shall permit or facilitate its introduction into Pakistan in any form.

(2)   All forms of forced labour and traffic in human beings are prohibited.

(3)   No child below the age of fourteen years shall be engaged in any factory or mine or any other hazardous employment.

---

[1]   Added by the Constitution (Third Amdt.) Act, 1975 (22 of 1975), s. 2.
[2]   New Article 10 A ins. by the Constitution (Eighteenth Amdt.) Act, 2010 (10 of 2010), s. 5.

(4)   Nothing in this Article shall be deemed to affect compulsory service

(a)   by any person undergoing punishment for an offence against any law; or

(b)   required by any law for public purpose:

Provided that no compulsory service shall be of a cruel nature or incompatible with human dignity.

Protection against retrospective punishment

12.   (1)   No law shall authorize the punishment of a person—

(a)   for an act or omission that was not punishable by law at the time of the act or omission; or

(b)   for an offence by a penalty greater than, or of a kind different from, the penalty prescribed by law for that offence at the time the offence was committed.

(2)   Nothing in clause (1) or in Article 270 shall apply to any law making acts of abrogation or subversion of a Constitution in force in Pakistan at any time since the twenty-third day of March, one thousand nine hundred and fifty-six, an offence.

Protection against double punishment and self incrimination

13.   No person—

(a)   shall be prosecuted or punished for the same offence more than once; or

(b)   shall, when accused of an offence, be compelled to be a witness against himself.

Inviolability of dignity of man, etc.

14.   (1)   The dignity of man and, subject to law, the privacy of home, shall be inviolable.

(2)   No person shall be subjected to torture for the purpose of extracting evidence.

Freedom of movement, etc.

15. Every citizen shall have the right to remain in, and, subject to any reasonable restriction imposed by law in the public interest, enter and move freely throughout Pakistan and to reside and settle in any part thereof.

Freedom of assembly

16. Every citizen shall have the right to assemble peacefully and without arms, subject to any reasonable restrictions imposed by law in the interest of public order.

Freedom of association

[17.] (1) Every citizen shall have the right to form associations or unions, subject to any reasonable restrictions imposed by law in the interest of sovereignty or integrity of Pakistan, public order or morality.

(2) Every citizen, not being in the service of Pakistan, shall have the right to form or be a member of a political party, subject to any reasonable restrictions imposed by law in the interest of the sovereignty or integrity of Pakistan and such law shall provide that where the Federal Government declares that any political party has been formed or is operating in a manner prejudicial to the sovereignty or integrity of Pakistan, the Federal Government shall, within fifteen days of such declaration, refer the matter to the Supreme Court whose decision on such reference shall be final.

(3) Every political party shall account for the source of its funds in accordance with law.]

Freedom of trade, business or profession

18. Subject to such qualifications, if any, as may be prescribed by law, every citizen shall have the right to enter upon any lawful profession or occupation, and to conduct any lawful trade or business:

Provided that nothing in this Article shall prevent—

(a) the regulation of any trade or profession by a licensing system; or

(b) the regulation of trade, commerce or industry in the interest of free competition therein; or

---

[1] Subs. by the Constitution (Eighteenth Amdt.) Act, 2010 (10 of 2010), s. 6.for –Article 17".

(c)   the carrying on, by the Federal Government or a Provincial Government, or by a corporation controlled by any such Government, of any trade, business, industry or service, to the exclusion, complete or partial, of other persons.

Freedom of speech, etc.

19. Every citizen shall have the right to freedom of speech and expression, and there shall be freedom of the press, subject to any reasonable restrictions imposed by law in the interest of the glory of Islam or the integrity, security or defence of Pakistan or any part thereof, friendly relations with foreign States, public order, decency or morality, or in relation to contempt of court, [1][commission of] or incitement to an offence.

Right to information.

[2][**19A.** Every citizen shall have the right to have access to information in all matters of public importance subject to regulation and reasonable restrictions imposed by law].

Freedom to profess religion and to manage religious institutions

20. Subject to law, public order and morality,—

(a)   every citizen shall have the right to profess, practice and propagate his religion; and

(b)   every religious denomination and every sect thereof shall have the right to establish, maintain and manage its religious institutions.

Safeguard against taxation for purposes of any particular religion

21. No person shall be compelled to pay any special tax the proceeds of which are to be spent on the propagation or maintenance of any religion other than his own.

---

[1] Subs. by the Constitution (Fourth Amdt.) Act, 1975 (71 of 1975), s. 4, for "defamation" (*w.e.f* the 21st November, 1975).
[2] New Article 19A ins. by the Constitution (Eighteenth Amdt.) Act, 2010 (10 of 2010), s. 7.

Safeguards as to educational institutions in respect of religion, etc.

22. (1) No person attending any educational institution shall be required to receive religious instruction, or take part in any religious ceremony, or attend religious worship, if such instruction, ceremony or worship relates to a religion other than his own.

(2) In respect of any religious institution, there shall be no discrimination against any community in the granting of exemption or concession in relation to taxation.

(3) Subject to law,

(a) no religious community or denomination shall be prevented from providing religious instruction for pupils of that community or denomination in any educational institution maintained wholly by that community or denomination; and

(b) no citizen shall be denied admission to any educational institution receiving aid from public revenues on the ground only of race, religion, caste or place of birth.

(4) Nothing in this Article shall prevent any public authority from making provision for the advancement of any socially or educationally backward class of citizens.

Provision as to property

23. Every citizen shall have the right to acquire, hold and dispose of property in any part of Pakistan, subject to the Constitution and any reasonable restrictions imposed by law in the public interest.

Protection of property rights

24. (1) No person shall be deprived of his property save in accordance with law.

(2) No property shall be compulsorily acquired or taken possession of save for a public purpose, and save by the authority of law which provides for compensation therefor and either fixes the amount of compensation or specifies the principles on and the manner in which compensation is to be determined and given.

(3)   Nothing in this Article shall affect the validity of—

(a) any law permitting the compulsory acquisition or taking possession of any property for preventing danger to life, property or public health; or

(b) any law permitting the taking over of any property which has been acquired by, or come into the possession of, any person by any unfair means, or in any manner, contrary to law; or

(c) any law relating to the acquisition, administration or disposal of any property which is or is deemed to be enemy property or evacuee property under any law (not being property which has ceased to be evacuee property under any law); or

(d) any law providing for the taking over of the management of any property by the State for a limited period, either in the public interest or in order to secure the proper management of the property, or for the benefit of its owner; or

(e) any law providing for the acquisition of any class of property for the purpose of—

(i) providing education and medical aid to all or any specified class of citizens; or

(ii) providing housing and public facilities and services such as roads, water supply, sewerage, gas and electric power to all or any specified class of citizens; or

(iii)providing maintenance to those who, on account of unemployment, sickness, infirmity or old age, are unable to maintain themselves; or

(f) any existing law or any law made in pursuance of Article 253.

(4)   The adequacy or otherwise of any compensation provided for by any such law as is referred to in this Article, or determined in pursuance thereof, shall not be called in question in any court.

25A. Equality of citizens

25. (1) All citizens are equal before law and are entitled to equal protection of law.

(2) There shall be no discrimination on the basis of sex [1]*.

(3) Nothing in this Article shall prevent the State from making any special provision for the protection of women and children.

Right to education

[2][**25A.** The State shall provide free and compulsory education to all children of the age of five to sixteen years in such manner as may be determined by law.]

Non-discrimination in respect of access to public places

26. (1) In respect of access to places of public entertainment or resort, not intended for religious purposes only, there shall be no discrimination against any citizen on the ground only of race, religion, caste, sex, residence or place of birth.

(2) Nothing in clause (1) shall prevent the State from making any special provision for women and children.

Safeguard against discrimination in services

27. (1) No citizen otherwise qualified for appointment in the service of Pakistan shall be discriminated against in respect of any such appointment on the ground only of race, religion, caste, sex, residence or place of birth:

Provided that, for a period not exceeding [3][forty] years from the commencing day, posts may be reserved for persons belonging to any class or area to secure their adequate representation in the service of Pakistan:

Provided further that, in the interest of the said service, specified posts or services may be reserved for members of either sex if such posts or services entail the performance of duties and functions which cannot be adequately performed by members of the other sex [4][:]

---

[1] The word "alone" omitted by the Constitution (Eighteenth Amdt.) Act, 2010 (10 of 2010), s. 8.

[2] New Article 25A ins. *ibid.*, s. 9.

[3] Subs. and shall be deemed always to have been so subs. by the Constitution (Sixteenth Amendment) Act, 1999 (7 of 1999), s. 2, for "twenty", which was previously subs. by P.O. No. 14 of 1985, Art. 2 and Sch., for "ten".

[4] Subs. by the Constitution (Eighteenth Amdt.) Act, 2010 (10 of 2010), s. 10 for the full-stop.

CPSIA information can be obtained
at www.ICGtesting.com
Printed in the USA
FFHW021957130120
57777660-63067FF

9 781480 884090